Birnbaum's

Tom Passavant
Editorial Director

Deanna Caron
Elisa Gallaro
Pamela S. Weiers
Senior Editors

Todd Sebastian Williams
Associate Art Director

Steve Ferazani
Miranda Spencer
Contributing Editors

Alexandra Mayes Birnbaum
Consulting Editor

HYPERION AND HEARST BUSINESS PUBLISHING, INC.

ISBN: 0-7868-8195-X

Printed in the United States of America

An enormous debt of gratitude is owed to Diane Hancock, Mariella Ure, Richard Gregorie, Laura Simpson, Julie Woodward, Gene Duncan, David Malvin, Bob Tucker, Alec Scribner, Ed Grier, Nancy Tucker, Kristine Dobson, Fred Trusty, Betsy Singer, LouAnne Cappiello, Kelli Gilbert, Hermina Fisher, Doreen Bjorn, Tya Ward, Mickey Metz, and Bob Mervine, all of whom performed above and beyond the call of duty to make the creation of this book possible. To Phil Lengyel, Tom Elrod, Linda Warren, Bob Miller, and Charlie Ridgway, thank you for believing in this project in the first place. And to Wendy Lefkon, special thanks for taking it from idea to reality.

Other 1997 Birnbaum Travel Guides

Bahamas, and Turks & Caicos
Bermuda
Canada
Cancun/Cozumel & Isla Mujeres
Caribbean
Country Inns & Back Roads
Disneyland
Hawaii
Mexico
Miami & Ft. Lauderdale
United States
Walt Disney World
Walt Disney World Without Kids

CONTENTS

We Wrote

What a great year to visit Walt Disney World! You can help celebrate the 25th birthday of the home of Mickey Mouse, Space Mountain, and Tower of Terror. But once you get there, where should you start? What should you see first? And where should you and your family stay?

That's why we wrote this book—to answer your questions and help you plan the most awesome vacation in the World. We thought you would like a kids' perspective. So here's a guide written especially for kids, by the kids you see in the photos. There's even a special section to tell you all about the 25th anniversary celebration.

To create this book, kids traveled to Walt Disney World with us, the editors of *Birnbaum's Walt Disney World*. We took kids ages 8 to 14 to get opinions from each age group.

This Book!

We went on several trips with different groups of kids each year and did our best to see all the things we thought you'd like most. We also stood in line so we could tell you which attractions are worth the wait and which you might want to save for another time.

Since you won't have time to do it all, read the descriptions of the attractions and decide which ones you most want to see—and which you could live without. On the next few pages, we tell you a little bit about each of the kids who has participated in this project. This information will give you an idea of whose opinions might be most like your own.

One of our kid experts, Tate, says, "I hope kids who read this book will appreciate my opinions and use them to make their trip as fun and exciting as possible."

We went on the most popular attractions twice, with different groups of kids to get a variety of opinions. The kids didn't always agree about each attraction. Even those who were the same age sometimes disagreed. You may have yet another opinion. Even so, the kids' ideas should help you decide how best to plan your trip.

During our visits, we spent many days touring the Magic Kingdom, Epcot, and the Disney-MGM Studios. We visited Fort Wilderness, ate in a lot of restaurants, and stopped by many of the hotels on the Disney grounds. We even had a chance to participate in a behind-the-scenes program.

Each year, we take new kids to check out the latest attractions. This year we saw Alien Encounter, the scariest show in the World, and watched Buzz Lightyear and Woody in their Toy Story Parade. We also returned to some of the kids' favorites—The Twilight Zone Tower of Terror, Innoventions, and Honey, I Shrunk the Audience. Once again, they were a big hit.

These are the big kids who had a great time helping to put this book together.

1 9 9 7

Emma Peters-Axtell

Emma, who lives in Duluth, Minnesota, was 9 years old when she worked on this book. She is on the editorial board of the *New Moon* magazine published in her home town. She also likes to sing and dance.

Brian Foster

Brian, who lives in Woodinville, Washington, was 10 years old when he worked on this book. He enjoys all kinds of sports, and likes to work on computers. He also collects coins and rocks.

Ashley Johnson

Ashley, who lives in Burbank, California, was 12 years old when she worked on this book. She's an actress who has been in many television shows, including "Growing Pains." She has nine pets.

Adam Farkas

Adam, who lives in Miami Beach, Florida, was 12 years old when he worked on this book. His favorite sports are hockey and football. He also enjoys hiking, rock climbing, and waterskiing.

The kids also enjoyed checking out the new restaurants, especially Chef Mickey's in the Contemporary resort. But the most exciting parts of the trip were the sneak previews of coming attractions—the 25th Anniversary Parade and Epcot's spectacular thrill ride, Test Track. The kids got a special look so they could tell you all about it.

All the kids who have worked on this guide agree that a week-long stay isn't enough. If you really want to see all that Walt Disney World has to offer, the kids suggest you plan on spending 1½ to 2 weeks.

Altogether, we spent almost 22 days and covered most of Walt Disney World, but we still have more to see. Walt Disney World is always changing and new things are added each year. So don't try to do everything in one trip. We'll be going back again to see what we missed, too. Next time we'll take different kids to see the newest attractions as well as all the old favorites, so you'll have even more opinions to consider.

The book is organized into six sections. The first covers the special events planned for the 25th anniversary celebration. The next three sections tell you about the theme parks. We describe each attraction, and then the kids offer their opinions. The fifth section covers places like the water parks,

Don't Forget to Write to Us!

Walt Disney World For Kids, By Kids
1790 Broadway, 6th Floor
New York, NY 10019

the hotels and restaurants, and other activities and attractions not in the parks. The last section is filled with hot tips from the kids on how to make your vacation even better.

Lots of things make this book interactive. There are places to put your own photos. The last page is ready for autographs. There's also space to make your lists of the attractions you most want to see and a section where you can plan your schedule.

We can't wait to hear what you think. So please write to us at the address above with your tips for the best vacation in the World.

Have a great trip!

Justin Berfield, '95

Justin, who lives in Oak Park, California, was 8 years old when he worked on this book. He's an actor, and has appeared in commercials, movies, and a television show. He loves animals and has some unusual pets.

Robert Raack, '94

Robert, who lives in Eugene, Oregon, was 8 years old when he worked on this book. He is very interested in dragons, and likes to play video games and soccer.

Lindsay Compton, '95 & '96

Lindsay, who lives in Dallas, Texas, was 9 the first year she worked on this book. She is a Girl Scout and also likes to play soccer and basketball. She loves to draw and wants to be an animal doctor someday.

Taran Noah Smith, '94

Taran was 9 years old when he worked on this book. He plays Mark Taylor, the youngest son on the show "Home Improvement." When he's not on the set, he lives in San Rafael, California. He likes to sail and ride his mountain bike.

Bradley Sanchez, '95

Bradley, who lives in Independence, Missouri, was 10 years old when he worked on this book. He likes to play football and is a fan of the Kansas City Chiefs. He enjoys playing video games.

Danielle Gould, '95

Danielle, who lives in Potomac, Maryland, was 11 years old when she worked on this book. She enjoys reading and loves to dance. She takes ballet, jazz, and tap lessons.

Ashley Pletz, '94

Ashley, who lives in Chicago, Illinois, was 11 years old when she worked on this book. She loves to write. She also takes ballet lessons and has done some modeling.

Elisabeth Woodhams, '94

Lissy, who lives in Tucson, Arizona, was 11 years old when she worked on this book. She plays the piano, is a member of a drama club, and enjoys horseback riding and swimming.

Dawna Boone, '95 & '96

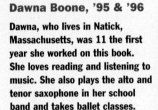

Dawna, who lives in Natick, Massachusetts, was 11 the first year she worked on this book. She loves reading and listening to music. She also plays the alto and tenor saxophone in her school band and takes ballet classes.

Brian Levinthal, '94

Brian, who lives in Huntington, New York, was 12 years old when he worked on this book. He is studying cartoon art, and plays the clarinet in the school band. He also likes to swim.

Anna Kerlek, '95

Anna, who lives in Chagrin Falls, Ohio, was 13 years old when she worked on this book. She is on her school volleyball, basketball, and track teams, and she loves to sing and play the piano.

Tate Lynche, '95 & '96

Tate was 13 the first year he worked on this book, and was a Mouseketeer on "The Mickey Mouse Club" show. He lives in St. Petersburg, Florida. He wants to be an entertainer, and he also enjoys in-line skating.

David Bickel, '94

David, who lives in Columbus, Ohio, was 13 years old when he worked on this book. He is a major sports fan and enjoys playing baseball and video games. His favorite teams are the Atlanta Braves and the Chicago Bulls.

Karyn Williams, '94 & '96

Karyn, who lives in Orlando, Florida, was 13 the first year she worked on this book. She is an aspiring actress. She also loves to travel, and once spent several weeks studying marine biology in Australia.

Adam Winchester, '95

Adam, who was 14 years old when he worked on this book, lives in Colorado Springs, Colorado. His favorite sports are hockey, basketball, baseball, and soccer. He hopes to become an architect or to work with computers.

Thomanita Booth, '94

Nita, who lives in Chesapeake, Virginia, was 14 years old when she worked on this book. She was a Mouseketeer on the "Mickey Mouse Club" show, and a member of the music group MMC. Nita also sings in her church choir.

The 25th Anniversary

Happy Birthday Walt Disney World! The Magic Kingdom is turning 25, and you're invited to the party. It's the biggest bash yet, with a huge cake and lots of decorations.

The first kids to visit Walt Disney World are probably about as old as your parents now. Those kids saw a very different place. No Epcot. No Disney-MGM Studios. No water parks. Just the Magic Kingdom. But back then there was nothing else like it. And that's even more true today.

Walt Disney World has grown more magical each year. There's a lot to celebrate, so 1997 is a very special year to visit. The party begins on October 1, 1996 and continues for all of 1997. The whole World is joining in, but the Magic Kingdom is having the most fun of all. Turn the page to find out what they've got planned for you. And save us some cake!

25th Anniversary Celebration

Cinderella Castle Cake

The castle has a new look for the anniversary celebration. It's decorated as a giant birthday cake, with bright pink icing and lots of candy trimmings. On top and all around are 25 candles—one for each year—that are lighted every night.

Want to Stay Out Late?

The Magic Kingdom usually stays open late only during the summer and on holidays. But for the 25th anniversary, it's open until dark all year long. That gives you more time to ride your favorite attractions. You can also see the Fantasy in the Sky fireworks and the SpectroMagic parade here any night of the year.

25th Anniversary Parade

Every character you can imagine is dancing down Main Street in Walt Disney World's first interactive parade. That means kids get to participate in lots of different ways.

The parade has six floats, each with its own music and character theme. They stop eight times along the way to perform mini shows featuring kids who are visiting the park that day. Volunteers are chosen at random along the parade route about 45 minutes before starting time. If you're picked, you might get to dance with Cinderella, play "Genie Says," or even keep the beat on the bongo drums.

We saw a special preview of this parade, so the kids could tell you about it. All agree with Adam F., who says, "This parade is a lot better than all the other ones I've seen because it's more interactive."

The first float stars all of the characters who've been around since the beginning. There's Mickey

and Minnie, Donald and Goofy, Chip 'n' Dale, and their pals. Cinderella rides along in her coach.

Next is *Beauty and the Beast*. Look for Belle and her enchanted friends as they dance with guests from the crowd. One of the kids' favorites is *The Little Mermaid* float, which squirts water while Sebastian's band plays "Under the Sea." Brian F. likes how "the crabs and the fish sing and play instruments." Emma says, "You can conga with all the different colored fish."

A huge Genie heads up the *Aladdin* float and leads a game of "Genie Says." Aladdin and Jasmine are along for the ride—on top of Abu, transformed into an elephant. The sound of drums tells you *The Lion King* float can't be far behind. "It's a jungle full of drums and animals," says Ashley J. "At every stop, they release 20 doves."

The last float has all the rest of your favorite characters in an enchanted forest. "It's a great forest, with every character they could fit," Emma says. Fireworks burst 30 feet in the air from a mini castle on the float.

IllumiNations 25

Since the Magic Kingdom can't have *all* the fun, Epcot's dazzling show has even more lasers and fireworks than usual. The new show is set to festive music from around the world. The best part is the "Circle of Life" finale. A special fireworks display creates a colorful birthday cake in the sky above the lagoon.

Magical Milestones

Walt Disney World has grown up a lot in 25 years.
Check out the chart below to see what's
been added—and when.

1996—Mickey's Toontown Fair

1995—Alien Encounter

1994—Tower of Terror

1992—Splash Mountain

1990—Star Tours

1989—Disney-MGM Studios

1988—Mickey's Birthdayland, Magic Kingdom's seventh land

1986—Captain EO 3-D movie

1984—Morocco pavilion

1982—Epcot

1980—Big Thunder Mountain Railroad

1976—River Country, first water park

1974—Space Mountain

1973—Pirates of the Caribbean

1971—Magic Kingdom Grand Opening

Magic Kingdom

The Magic Kingdom is the most enchanting part of Walt Disney World, especially during this 25th anniversary year. Most people hear the words Walt Disney World and immediately picture the soaring towers of Cinderella Castle. They'll look much different during 1997, when the castle is decorated as an enormous birthday cake. Look for other special anniversary touches as you explore the Magic Kingdom.

Kids can spend lots of time in the seven "lands"—Main Street, Adventureland, Frontierland, Liberty Square, Fantasyland, Mickey's Toontown Fair, and Tomorrowland. The park is packed with attractions, so plan ahead and set an order to visit them. This chapter can help you decide which attractions you most want to see. Then make a list of the ones that fall into your "second choice" category and a list of the things you can live without. That way you can organize your visit and avoid wasting time.

While you're here, notice the little details that make the place so special. The theme of each land is shown in the costumes worn by the people who work there and the design of the shops and restaurants.

Main Street, U.S.A.

This is the Disney version of how a small-town Main Street would have looked around the year 1900. And it's perfect down to the last detail. There are hitching posts where townspeople would have tied up their horses and many other touches that make this Main Street so attractive. Crews of painters keep the buildings looking fresh. There are no major attractions on Main Street, but the 25th Anniversary Parade comes past here each afternoon. There are also a few other interesting things to see.

Walt Disney World Railroad

Walt Disney was a big train buff. He even built a model railroad in his backyard! The trains that run on the Walt Disney World Railroad are real locomotives that were originally built around 1900. Disney Imagineers found them in Mexico in 1969. The trains have been completely overhauled, and all their parts have been replaced.

A ride on the railroad gives a quick overview of the Magic Kingdom. The full round trip takes about 20 minutes, but you can get on and off at any of the stations. Main Street is the starting point and ending point. In between, trains make stops in Frontierland and Mickey's Toontown Fair.

The kids agree that the train is a nice way to travel around the park. "It's a great way to get around

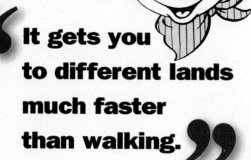

Shopping

Main Street, U.S.A. is lined with many different shops. There are places to buy candy, clothing, souvenirs, hats, cameras, and jewelry. Shops stay open a half hour after the park closes to give you a little extra time. Shopping tips are on page 146 in the *Everything Else in the World* chapter.

" **It gets you to different lands much faster than walking.** "

David
(age 13)

without walking, and the sights are nice, too," says Karyn. David agrees. "It gets you to different lands much faster than walking."

Main Street Cinema

Ever wonder how Mickey Mouse became a star? You'll find the answer in *Mickey's Big Break*, the short film shown in this theater. You'll also get to see Mickey in one of his early roles in a classic cartoon. There are no seats, so don't stop here if you're tired.

"There's a big difference between the movies Disney used to put out and the ones they do now," says Dawna. Adam F. agrees. "The old cartoon was kind of neat. It was the

first one with sound," he says. Tate also thinks "it's nice to see Mickey's beginnings."

The kids agree that the cinema is a bit boring. Brian F. says, "I just don't think this is for kids." Ashley J.'s advice sums it up: "If you're on a tight schedule, don't go see this."

Adventureland

Adventureland combines the exotic islands of the Caribbean, Polynesia, and Southeast Asia. The landscaping features many plants and trees native to these islands. The buildings look like ones you might see if you traveled there. Adventureland has four main attractions—Pirates of the Caribbean, the Jungle Cruise, the Swiss Family Treehouse, and the Tropical Serenade.

Pirates of the Caribbean

See a pirate raid on a Caribbean island town as you float through this adventure. Cannons fire into the air while pirates attack and pillage a village. The song "Yo Ho, Yo Ho; a Pirate's Life for Me" is the ride's catchy theme. As you make your way through the different scenes, pay attention to details like the exploding flowerpots and the interesting face of each pirate. Near the end, don't miss the pirate with his leg dangling over the bridge—the leg is actually hairy.

There's one small flume drop during the ride, so be prepared.

"This is an excellent ride," says David. "My favorite part is the pirate ship with the wind blowing and all the cannons firing. And I love how the characters look real."

Karyn thinks the details are great, too. "I was really paying attention to things like the hair on that guy's leg, the pirate chasing the lady, and the fire—it all just looks so real," she says. Ashley P. notices the characters, also. "The costumes are neat," she says.

But Lissy thinks the ride is a little dull. "It's really slow and I'm not that into pirates, so it doesn't amuse me too much." Brian L. agrees. "It isn't as exciting as I thought it would be," he says.

> **"It all just looks so real."**
> Karyn (age 13)

"I do like all the details and the way things look very realistic—especially the pirate's hairy leg."

Nita's favorite part is the dip. "There should be more dips, but it's still a cool ride," she says.

Robert agrees. "My favorite part has to be the drop," he says. "I thought the pirate was pointing his gun right at me—that's cool. The only part I'm not crazy about is the skull and crossbones. It's too dark."

> **"I thought the pirate was pointing his gun right at me—that's cool."**
> Robert (age 8)

Jungle Cruise

Become an explorer on this journey through four far-away lands—a Southeast Asian jungle, the Nile valley, the African grasslands, and the Amazon rain forest. Along the way you'll see elephants, zebras, giraffes, lions, hippos, and even headhunters. The captain of the ship tells lots of corny jokes, which can affect how much you enjoy the ride. This attraction is usually very crowded. Ask if the wait is more than 15 minutes. If it is, come back another time.

Some of the kids think the ride is a little dull. "There isn't enough action in it," says David. "It would be neat if you got wet."

Nita agrees. "I think it's boring and not a good ride for teenagers," she says. "I'd recommend it if you have nothing better to do on a hot day."

Karyn thinks the Jungle Cruise is a "nice family ride. But the guide has a lot to do with how much you like it, and our guide wasn't very good." Ashley P. agrees. "I did not like our guide. His jokes were really stupid," she says.

Don't wait more than 15 minutes for this ride.

Lissy and Robert like the Jungle Cruise. "The driver let me drive the boat for a while and that was really fun," says Lissy. "I like the way all the fake animals look real."

Robert agrees. "I love the ride," he says. "It would be even cooler if the headhunters really threw their spears."

Swiss Family Treehouse

Before you go see the treehouse, it's a good idea to know something about the classic story of the Swiss Family Robinson. The Robinsons were traveling to New Guinea when their ship was wrecked on an island during a storm. Mr. Robinson and two of his three sons built a treehouse. Although the family was given several chances to leave the island, all but one son decided to stay. The treehouse was so comfortable that the family had "everything we need right at our fingertips," said Mr. Robinson.

Disney's version of the treehouse has many levels that you climb by way of a staircase. There are quilts on the beds, and there's running water in every room. The tree is a creation of the Walt Disney World props department. It has 300,000 plastic leaves. Its concrete roots are set 42 feet into the ground.

Everyone agrees that reading the story or seeing the Disney movie about the Swiss Family Robinson makes the treehouse much more fun to explore.

> **"Once you know the story, then the treehouse is fascinating. "**
>
> David
> (age 13)

"You have to know the story to understand it," says Karyn. "It's so neat after you know what you're looking at. My favorite room is the kitchen," she adds.

"Once you know the story, then the treehouse is fascinating," says David. "I like the boys' room with the hammocks and the running water."

Lissy agrees. "You wouldn't know why they built the treehouse in the first place. They did a good job of disguising it because it looks like a real tree."

Ashley P. likes the treehouse and says "the kitchen is my favorite."

Try to read the book or see the movie about the Swiss Family Robinson before you visit this attraction.

Robert has seen the movie and read the book, so he really understood what he was seeing. "I could name all the rooms as we walked around," he says. "It's an excellent treehouse."

Tropical Serenade

Here's your chance to see the very first Walt Disney World attraction with Audio-Animatronics figures. Your hosts are José, Michael, Pierre, and Fritz. They introduce you to more than 200 birds, flowers, and tiki statues that sing and whistle a variety of songs.

The kids agree that this attraction is a little silly and outdated. But they do think it's interesting to see the early Audio-Animatronics figures and compare them with the newer ones.

"It's just a bunch of singing birds," says Lindsay. Brad thinks the songs go "too fast. It's hard to understand what they're saying."

For Dawna, "It doesn't matter how old you are, you will find this very boring. And it's too long."

Danielle and Anna, however, found things to like here. "The scenery is really pretty," says Danielle. Anna adds, "It's cool how the birds, flowers, and figures move their beaks and bodies with the words."

Frontierland

Frontierland represents the American Frontier—from New England to the Southwest—from the 1770s to the 1880s. It includes two of the most popular attractions in the park. Both are mountains. You can take a watery trip down Splash Mountain and ride a runaway train at Big Thunder Mountain Railroad. Other attractions in Frontierland include the Country Bear Jamboree, the Diamond Horseshoe Saloon Revue, the Frontierland Shootin' Arcade, and Tom Sawyer Island.

Splash Mountain

This is the newest peak in the Magic Kingdom mountain range. You must be at least 44 inches tall to ride. At Splash Mountain, you travel in a log boat through brightly painted scenes from Walt Disney's movie, *Song of the South*. You'll see Brer Rabbit, Brer Fox, and Brer Bear getting into all kinds of trouble. There are three smaller dips during the ride, all leading up to the big drop—a sharp plunge down 52 feet going

Hot Tip

Sit in the front if you want to get wet.

40 miles per hour. If you're sitting in the front of the log, you get very wet. If you're in the back, you just get a small splash.

"It's really cool," says Taran. "The last drop is awesome!" Ashley P. likes "all the dips, but the last one is great. I like how my belly would flip-flop on the way down."

Brad loves getting wet. "When you're in the front, you get all drenched," he says. Lissy didn't get as wet. "The big drop is awesome, but you don't get too wet if you're sitting in the back of the log."

The kids agree that you have to go on the ride a few times before you can appreciate the scenery and the story about Brer Rabbit, Brer Bear,

20

"When you're in the front, you get all drenched."

Brad (age 10)

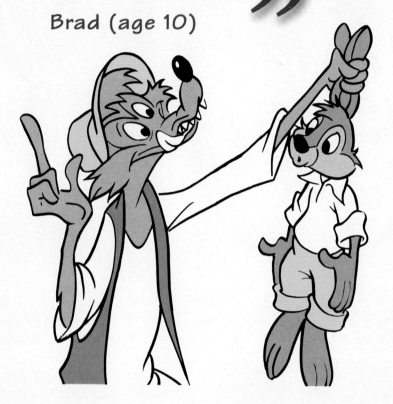

and Brer Fox. "The dips are incredible," says Brian L. "But I didn't know what was going on inside the mountain." Lissy agrees. "I didn't know the story until I heard the song 'Zip-A-Dee-Doo-Dah.' Then I knew where it was from."

Some of the kids were able to catch some of the details of the story. Lindsay says, "As it goes slow, you can see all the scenery. Every time there's a little splash, something different happens to

Brer Rabbit." Brad agrees. "I love that story. Brer Rabbit is supposed to be in the log getting away from the fox and the bear."

Robert thinks "the scenery is really good, especially at the end when Brer Fox gets his tail pulled by an alligator." Tate says, "You really need to look at the story. It makes the ride even better."

Karyn agrees. "All the characters are so cute and so detailed, and of course, the last drop is great."

Country Bear Jamboree

At this country-and-western show, about 20 lifesize Audio-Animatronics bears sing songs, play musical instruments, and tell a few jokes. It's a silly show, so it's important to go in with a silly attitude. Big Al, one of the most popular bears, can't even carry a tune.

The show gets mixed reviews from the kids, with most of them not enthusiastic.

"It's strictly for little kids ages 2 to 6," says Lissy. "It's a serious waste of time for older kids."

Karyn agrees, giving the show a rating of "two thumbs down and a couple of toes. But I think little kids would like to sing along with the characters," she adds.

"The show is very boring," says David. "I hate country music, so I really don't like this show."

Still, some of the kids find something to like. For example, Ashley P. says she hates the show, "but the little bear that is unhappy and squeaks is kind of cute."

Brian L. thinks, "The bears are great, and some of them are very funny. The one that seems to be drunk and can't sing is really funny. I think the show is very enjoyable."

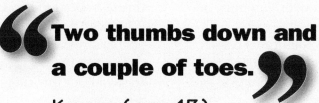

Big Thunder Mountain Railroad

Ride a roller coaster that races inside and outside Big Thunder Mountain. There are enough swoops and turns to keep this trip thrilling, but it's tamer than Space Mountain. You must be at least 40 inches tall to ride.

The runaway mine trains pass through several scenes with some real-looking chickens, donkeys, and goats. This is a ride you can go on again and again, and still find new things to see each time. It's also a good ride to try once during the day and once at night. In the daytime, try to catch all the details of the flooded mining town. Look for the rainmaker and the man dressed in long johns as he spins through the flood in a bathtub. See if you can spot the party going on upstairs in the saloon.

The kids have only good things to say about this ride. "It's full of

I would ride it again and again.

Danielle (age 11)

twists and turns," says Tate. Justin says, "I like all the turns. It's not too scary, but I was screaming because it's so much fun."

Adam W. says, "I love how there's a mining town down below. Don't miss the donkey wagging its tail." Lindsay also notices that "the background stuff is set up really nice. And I like that you feel like the ride is over, but then you go down another hill."

Anna thinks it's a great ride. "There are no huge drops, and it goes just fast enough to get a thrill. The scenery is great, too."

Danielle calls it "tame but really, really fun. I would ride it again and again."

PASTE A MAGIC KINGDOM PHOTO HERE

Read *The Adventures of Tom Sawyer* before visiting this island.

Tom Sawyer Island

To reach Tom Sawyer Island, you take a raft ride across the Rivers of America. The island has a working windmill, hills to climb, and two neat bridges. One is a swing bridge and the other is a barrel bridge. When one person bounces, everybody does. Across the bridges is Fort Sam Clemens, where there's a guardhouse with a bunch of Audio-Animatronics animals. The second floor of the fort has air guns that you can shoot.

"I kept jumping on the bridges," says Justin. "I also like the cave and the fort where you get to shoot

out." Brad also had fun with the rifles. "I like pretending that I'm shooting something. I like the raft ride over, too."

Dawna recommends reading *The Ad entures of Tom Sawyer* before visiting the island. "I think you have to read the book to understand the whole story. I like the raft ride over to the island because in the book, Tom takes a raft," she says.

Some of the older kids think the island is a little boring. "The bridges and caves are fun, but the rest is boring," says Adam W. Tate agrees. "I thought it would be a big play place for kids since Tom Sawyer is a kid like us, but I don't think it's very special."

At the **Frontierland Shootin' Arcade**, you can fire rifles that send infrared beams at targets. Hit the tombstones and they rise, sink, and spin. Hit the gravedigger's shovel, and a skull pops out of the grave. You have to pay extra to use the arcade. It's not included in your park admission.

An energetic crew of singers and dancers performs all day at the **Diamond Horseshoe Saloon Revue**. The jokes are very corny, but the performers are entertaining.

Liberty Square

Liberty Square is a small area that separates Frontierland from Fantasyland. It's a quiet spot with several shops and a couple of the Magic Kingdom's most popular attractions—The Haunted Mansion and The Hall of Presidents. The Liberty Square Riverboat is another attraction found here.

The Haunted Mansion

There are so many special effects inside The Haunted Mansion that you can go through it over and over again, and still not catch them all. It's not too scary, but there are plenty of surprises to keep you on your toes. When you enter the building, you're led into a hall where the host gives you an idea of what you're in for. The ceiling starts to rise and the walls begin to stretch— or at least that's how it seems. You're actually in an elevator that helps create these special effects. There's a moment before you board your "Doom Buggy" when the room is completely dark. It only lasts about 15 seconds, but for kids who are afraid of the dark, that's much too long.

Once on board your buggy, there are so many things to see. Watch for the raven that appears over and over again, the door knockers that knock themselves, the ghostly teapot pouring tea, and the dancing ghosts.

"It's awesome!" says Lissy. "It's kind of scary because you never know what's going to come next. It's very surprising."

Dawna agrees. "I like how they have things popping out at you. And the dancing ghosts look so real." Danielle adds, "The special effects are great."

> **It's awesome! You never know what's going to come next.**
>
> Lissy
> (age 11)

"If you don't like the dark, this is not a ride for you."

Robert (age 8)

David thinks younger kids may be frightened by the ride. "Older kids understand there's no such thing as ghosts," he says. Justin likes The Haunted Mansion but warns, "If you get scared easily, don't go."

Robert thinks that's good advice. "It's fun at the start, but then it gets pitch black and it's too scary," he says. "If you don't like the dark, this is not a ride for you."

But Lindsay still enjoyed the ride. "The man at the beginning tried to make it sound scary," she says. "When you actually go on the ride, it's not too spooky."

The Hall of Presidents

The first part of this attraction is an interesting film that discusses the importance of the Constitution from the time it was written through the beginning of the Space Age. A famous poet, Maya Angelou, is the narrator.

Then the screen rises and all of the presidents, from George Washington to Bill Clinton, are represented by Audio-Animatronics figures. The

Abraham Lincoln and Bill Clinton figures make speeches. Be sure to watch all the presidents closely because they move around, whisper to the person next to them, and shake hands.

The kids were pleasantly surprised by this attraction. Danielle says, "I thought it would be boring, but it isn't. It's very interesting." Lindsay agrees. "It's a fun way to learn," she says.

Brad thinks "it's like being on a school field trip. The Audio-Animatronics presidents look

real, even though they're fake." Adam W. agrees. "The way they move makes it very realistic. I especially like Bill Clinton and Abraham Lincoln."

Justin likes that "it teaches about the presidents. A lot of the names I had never heard before." Dawna points out that "people usually know about George Washington, Abraham Lincoln, and the current president, but not anyone in between." She also likes all the costumes.

The kids agree that when each president's name is announced, the spotlight on him should be brighter. Then it would be easier to find each president on stage.

The **Liberty Square Riverboat**, named *Richard F. Irvine* after a Disney designer, is a real steamboat. The ride is slow, but it's a nice break on a hot afternoon. The best seats are right up front or in the back, where you can see both sides of the Rivers of America as you go along.

The way they move makes it very realistic.

Adam W. (age 14)

Mickey's Toontown Fair

Even Disney characters need a place to get away from it all. That's why Mickey, Minnie, and friends have country homes in Mickey's Toontown Fair, the newest land in the Magic Kingdom. The best way to get there is aboard the Walt Disney World Railroad. You can also walk over from Fantasyland.

Everywhere you look, there are colorful tents. That's because the county fair is always in town—and Mickey is the head judge. Visit **Mickey's Country House** and see his judge outfit, hanging neatly in his bedroom. Watch a broadcast of the fair on the TV in his living room. Check out his gameroom and Ping-Pong table. See the mess Donald and Goofy have made in the kitchen, which they're helping Mickey remodel.

Then, head out the back door to the **Judge's Tent** to meet Mickey. On your way, be sure to look at what's growing in his garden. Even the vegetables have ears!

Minnie's Country House is next door. It's a real treat for kids because there's lots to see and touch. And her foam furniture is

perfect for climbing. Pass through Minnie's Art Studio, where she creates all sorts of things to enter in the fair. Minnie's a great cook, painter, and gardener, so she wins a lot. In her Work Nook, she edits her very own magazine called *Minnie's Cartoon Living*. Her answering machine is in here, too. Press the button and listen to her messages.

The best spot in Minnie's house is the kitchen. The coffee pot is steaming, popcorn is popping, and a cake is rising in the oven. Open

Hot Tip

Mickey's Toontown Fair is the best place to meet the characters.

the refrigerator for a peek at her favorite cheeses, and feel the blast of cold air. Then go out back to meet Minnie in her garden gazebo. Minnie's garden is as interesting as Mickey's. It's filled with "tiger" lilies, "butter" cups, "two" lips, and dandy "lions."

Next head over to **Donald's Boat**. It's called the *Miss Daisy*, of course. Just walk across the "pond" to get there. But watch out for the water jets. Also, it seems that the boat has a few leaks. If you're like most kids, you'll think it's a great place to get wet.

The only ride in Toontown Fair is **The Barnstormer at Goofy's Wiseacres Farm**, a mini roller coaster. Young kids get to fly planes on a track that goes around the

farm and then crashes right through Goofy's barn! The hole in the barn is shaped just like Goofy, so you know he was the first to try the ride. Goofy also has some fun things for you to see while you wait in line. He's growing "pop" corn, and "bell" peppers, but something has flattened the squash. Don't miss the extra-high mailbox, designed especially for air mail.

Mickey's Toontown Fair Hall of Fame is a tent filled with all the winning entries from the fair. It's also the best spot to meet the characters, including old favorites like Goofy, Donald, and Chip 'n' Dale. There's a room with fairy-tale princesses and another with famous Disney villains.

One more place to stop is **Toon Park**, a playground with foam animals for young kids to climb on. Don't be fooled by **Pete's Garage**. It may look like a gas station, but it's really where you'll find the restrooms.

Fantasyland

Many of Walt Disney World's kiddie rides are in Fantasyland, but there are a few attractions that older kids and even grownups enjoy. We visited most of Fantasyland's rides during the 3 P.M. Main Street parade—and we suggest you do the same. These attractions are very popular, but the lines are much shorter while most people are at the parade. So it's a good idea to skip the parade one day to tour Fantasyland, and use the time to go on the rides. Catch the parade on another day.

Cinderella's Golden Carrousel

Just about all of the attractions at Walt Disney World were designed and built by Imagineers. The carousel is one exception. It was built around 1917. Imagineers discovered it in New Jersey, where it was once part of an amusement park.

When you climb on a horse for your ride on the carousel, be sure to notice that each one is different.

And remember to look up at the ceiling and its hand-painted scenes from *Cinderella*. While you ride, enjoy famous Disney tunes including "Zip-A-Dee-Doo-Dah," "When You Wish Upon A Star," and "Chim-Chim-Cheree."

"You can never grow too old for a carousel."

Lissy (age 11)

"I think you can never grow too old for a carousel," says Lissy. "The horses are beautiful and the music makes it great."

Robert agrees. "I love the carousel and I love the music. I think people of any age would like it."

Some of the other kids feel differently. "It's very boring and babyish," says Ashley P. David agrees. "I think it goes on forever and it's boring," he says.

Nita found a way to make the ride more fun for everyone by clapping in time with the music. "It's boring, so that's why I started clapping," she says. Brian L. thinks that helps a lot. "I didn't like it until we all started clapping," he says. "Then it was kind of fun."

Karyn thinks the carousel is a nice, relaxing ride. "It was fun when we all were clapping, and it's nice to just rest for a little while."

All the kids agree that they wouldn't wait in a long line to ride.

Don't Forget
If the line is long, save the carousel for another time.

Mad Tea Party

The idea for the oversize teacups that spin wildly through this ride was taken from a scene in *Alice In Wonderland*. In the movie, the Mad Hatter throws himself a tea party to celebrate his un-birthday.

On the Mad Tea Party ride, you control how fast your cup spins by turning the big wheel in the center. The more you turn, the more you spin. Or you can just sit back and let the cup spin on its own. It may be difficult while you're whirling, but try to take a peek at the little mouse who keeps popping out of the big teapot in the center.

"It's a very good ride and it really makes you dizzy," says Nita.

Brian L. agrees. "I wish it would go even faster, but it's good that you can go as fast or as slow as you want," he says. Ashley J. adds, "When you start spinning really fast, you start laughing really hard!"

Robert says, "The ride is really cool. I think it should have power steering, though."

For the best ride, David suggests that everyone in the cup try to work together. "You have to coordinate," he says. "Sometimes you can go faster if fewer people work at spinning the wheel."

All the kids agree about two things: The ride is too short (it lasts about two minutes), and it would be better if there were a button to push instead of the wheel to spin. "Your arms get tired after a while," says Lissy, "but the teacups are always fun."

Dumbo, the Flying Elephant

Just like the star of the movie *Dumbo*, the elephants at this attraction fly. You can climb aboard and take a short ride (about two minutes) up and over Fantasyland. A button lets you control the up and down movement of the elephant. Timothy Mouse, who becomes Dumbo's manager in the movie, sits on top of a mirrored ball in the middle of the flying elephants. The ride received a fresh coat of colorful paint not too long ago, and more Dumbos were added so that now more people can ride at once.

Many of the kids agree that this ride is more fun for younger kids from ages 3 to 8. But they all find something to like, and think it would be fun to go on with a younger brother or sister.

"I think it's great for younger kids," says Karyn. "It's pretty boring for kids my age, though." Brian L. also recommends it for younger kids. "It's not a bad ride and I think little kids would love it," he says. Anna thinks "it's way too short. But if you don't wait in line too long, it's fun to go on."

Lindsay says, "It needs to be new and improved again. But it's fun to control how high you go." Robert likes "to go up really high. I think some little kids might be scared of the height, though."

Danielle loves it. "It has the appearance of a child's ride, but it's fun for everyone," she says. Tate agrees. "Most people think it's just for little kids, but it's fun."

"It's fun for everyone."

Danielle (age 11)

Peter Pan's Flight

Swoop and soar through scenes that tell the story of how Wendy, Michael, and John get sprinkled with pixie dust, head for "the second star to the right and straight on till morning," and fly off to Never Land with Tinker Bell. Along the way they meet up with Princess Tiger Lily, the evil Captain Hook, and his sidekick Mr. Smee. Near the end of the trip, there's a beautiful scene of London at night. Notice that the cars on the streets really move. Also, watch out for the crocodile who's about to eat Captain Hook.

When you first board your pirate ship, it seems like you're riding on a track on the ground. Once you get going the track is actually above you, so you feel like you're really flying.

"I love this ride and how it makes you feel like you can fly," says Robert. "I especially like the part at the end with the crocodile."

Ashley P. thinks "the city scene is neat with all the cars going up and down. I also like how it's so dark."

"It really brings out the kid in you."

Nita (age 14)

Lissy enjoys "how you fly over all the scenes from the story. I really like the music, too." Nita says, "I think it really brings out the kid in you."

David points out that Peter Pan's Flight is different from all the other Fantasyland rides because "you're hooked from the top instead of being on a track below you." He adds, "I never get tired of this ride."

Brian L. likes all the details, like the costumes and colors of the characters. "I like how it shows parts from the movie *Peter Pan*," he says, "and I like it that you're flying instead of riding on the ground."

It's A Small World

This is a boat ride through a mini wonderland. Boats take you slowly through several large rooms where beautiful, Audio-Animatronics dolls represent different parts of the world. There are wooden soldiers, cancan dancers, Dutch children, Greek dancers, snake charmers, hot-air balloon fliers, leprechauns, bagpipers, and many more. There's even a jungle scene with hippos, giraffes, and monkeys.

All this colorful scenery is set to the song "It's A Small World," which plays over and over again. Pay attention to the detailed costumes on the dolls, and try to guess which country they're from. There are usually two lines at this attraction, and the one on the left is almost always shorter.

"I love all the costumes, the different dolls, and the customs," says Karyn. "Every time you go, you see something new." Nita says, "The costumes are adorable, and I like the expressions on the dolls. But the ride is too slow. If it had a few dips it would be better."

Lissy agrees that the ride is a little slow, but "it's really pretty and there are so many neat things to look at that it doesn't matter."

Ashley P. thinks the song gets a little tiring. "I really like the costumes and cultures, but the song just keeps playing over and over."

Brian L. says, "The figures are neat, and I love all the colors and costumes. The ride should be shorter, though."

As for David, "I don't hate it, but I do think it's better for younger kids," he says.

Mr. Toad's Wild Ride

Mr. Toad is not a very good driver. So when you hop into one of his cars heading to "Nowhere in Particular," you're in for a wild trip. The cars go zigging and zagging around sharp turns. You crash through a fireplace, just miss being hit by a falling suit of armor, go through haystacks and barn doors into a chicken coop, and then ride down a railroad track on a collision course with a speeding train.

Most of the kids agree that Mr. Toad's Wild Ride is for younger kids, although there are a few scary moments that might frighten them.

"It's good for younger kids," says Karyn. "It's pretty boring for someone my age."

David agrees that it's a kiddie ride. "Some of the characters are funny, but it's really just for younger kids," he says. "I don't like that the characters are all made out of cardboard."

But Lissy thinks the scenery is "neat and I like how they have everything moving. When I saw the train coming, it was a little scary," she says. Robert agrees. "It sort of scared me a little bit," he says.

Brian L. thinks the sound track is too loud. "The ride is good for younger kids, but the noise might scare them."

> **"Some of the characters are funny, but it's really just for younger kids."**
>
> David
> (age 13)

Snow White's Adventures

This attraction takes you through some of the scariest parts from the story of *Snow White and the Seven Dwarfs*. Snow White is in a lot of the scenes, but so is the witch. There are also Audio-Animatronics dwarfs. At the end of the ride, they wave to Snow White and her prince.

There are lots of turns, and that witch seems to be around each one of them. During most of the ride it's very dark, so it can get pretty scary—especially for younger children.

The kids agree that this attraction doesn't fit well into any age category. It's very scary for young children and a little boring for older kids.

"At least Snow White is in it, but I still think it's too scary for little kids," says Karyn. "If it's going to be a kiddie ride, there should be more happy parts in it." Tate says, "I expected something more."

Brian L. likes that some scenes are like the movie, but he agrees, "Little kids would be terrified seeing the wicked witch." Ashley P. likes the ride but thinks "the witch hops out so close to you."

Dawna says, "I like how we moved from scene to scene in our car. Still, I wouldn't wait in a long line for this ride."

Legend of
The Lion King

Walt Disney's smash hit comes to life in Legend of The Lion King. This show uses animation, lifesize puppets, special effects, and music to make you part of the world of Simba.

You start in the pre-show area, where you meet Rafiki, the wise baboon who narrates the story.

Soon the doors to the theater open, and you step into the scene of the Circle of Life. The sun rises over Pride Rock as Mufasa tells his son, Simba, that he will always have his father with him. The characters are fully automated puppets, whose heads, ears, and feet move, and whose mouths open and shut when they speak.

❝**I was mesmerized the whole time.**❞

Dawna (age 11)

As the story continues, you meet other characters from the movie and experience some of its most dramatic scenes. You're there when Mufasa is trampled and when Simba discovers that his father is dead. You see the evil Scar make Simba believe it's his fault his father has died. You go with Simba when he leaves the kingdom and finds freedom with Timon and Pumbaa. Later, you watch as he falls in love with Nala. When Rafiki convinces Simba it's time to go back to the kingdom, you return with him as he takes his place as The Lion King.

The special effects, like mists and winds, make it seem as if you're really in the jungle. During the stampede scene, feel the theater rumble as Mufasa is trampled by the wildebeests.

All the kids think this is a great show. "This has to be the best show anywhere," Dawna says.

"I was mesmerized the whole time." Lindsay calls it "a good performance, with all of your favorite songs and characters from the movie." Karyn says it's a "must-see." Even Tate, who's never seen *The Lion King* "thoroughly enjoyed it."

If you're a Lion King fan, don't miss the Fantasy Faire gift shop outside the show. Everything is based on the hit movie, so you're sure to find something you like.

Skyway to Tomorrowland

Get a bird's-eye view of the Magic Kingdom on the cable cars that run overhead between Fantasyland and Tomorrowland.

"This is fun," says Lindsay. "You get a really good view of the park and you can take pictures." Brad agrees. "It's cool going up in the air. You get to see everything."

Anna suggests that you "walk if the line is longer than ten minutes. It's silly to wait if you can get there faster." But Adam W. says, "It's nice to ride and rest your feet."

Dawna and Danielle both think the ride feels like a ski lift. Dawna offers this tip: "It's not a good ride if you're afraid of heights."

Board at Tomorrowland, where the lines are usually shorter.

notes

Tomorrowland

Tomorrowland was designed as Walt Disney World's version of the future. But the present keeps catching up, so most of the land was updated recently to look like a city from a science fiction story. One thing is still the same— Space Mountain, which is among the Magic Kingdom's most popular rides. Some of the newest attractions in the land are Alien Encounter, Astro Orbiter, and The Timekeeper.

Space Mountain

Roller coaster fans will want to head straight for Space Mountain and its fast, winding trip through the galaxy. You must be at least 44 inches tall to ride. You travel in a rocket, in the dark (but not pitch black), with stars and meteors all around.

The kids agree that the turns and pretty steep dips of Space Mountain make for a great ride. Justin thinks "it's fun because you never know what's going to happen next." All the special effects make the ride even better for Brad. "The speeding lights look really neat," he says.

Once you get inside the mountain, you choose between two lines. Karyn thinks "sitting on the left is better because there are more dips and turns."

The **Tomorrowland Light & Power Co.** is a video arcade located at the exit of Space Mountain. It's a great place to wait if you don't ride. Brian F. says, "This arcade is better than some others because there are a lot more games." One of the most popular games is the Sega Virtua Formula race car. "You get to sit in a simulated car," says Dawna. "It's almost like really driving in a race." As at most arcades, you'll have to pay to play.

Nita has a warning for kids who aren't sure if they want to go on: "It goes too fast for somebody like me. I'm not a roller coaster person, and I felt like I was about to fall out when it went sideways." Another bit of good advice from Lindsay: "Make

Hot Tip
Never eat right before going on Space Mountain.

sure you don't go on this ride right after you eat."

The ride lasts just over 2½ minutes. "Waiting in line you think 'The ride is only two minutes long! That's not long enough,'" says Lissy. "Then you get on and two minutes seems too long," she says.

All the kids agree that the ride is "good scary." Anything "bad scary" happened only in their imaginations. Anna says, "The ride rattles a lot. I wish that there were sides to the cars." But don't worry: The roller coaster is perfectly safe to go on as many times as you want. As Tate says, "Just one word—again!"

"You'll scream until you can scream no more!"

Ashley J. (age 12)

Alien Encounter

Visitors from another planet invite you to watch them demonstrate their company's new teleporter. This is a high-tech machine that can beam people through space. To show you exactly how it works, they try to beam their company president right into this theater in the Magic Kingdom. But something goes wrong: An ugly alien arrives instead and escapes into the audience.

That's the story behind Alien Encounter, the Magic Kingdom's scariest attraction. Special effects play a big part in this show. Smoke, sparks, and lots of sounds make things very frightening. You must be at least 7 years old and 48 inches tall to enter this attraction.

The kids like this show a lot, but stress that it's not for everyone—especially younger kids. Brian F. says, "I did not go on it, because I don't like aliens. I went to the arcade instead."

Lindsay is just the opposite. She likes scary things. "I love this show," she says. "The special effects are really cool. It's neat how they make the creature disappear and reappear somewhere else."

Adam F. also likes the special effects. "They show the alien in front of you. Then the lights flash off and you feel like it's breathing and slobbering on you." Emma calls Alien Encounter "thrilling. I give it the best rating it can get. It's like you almost get eaten by a monster, but you know it's just a ride. I screamed for the fun of it."

Ashley J. says, "When the alien gets out, you'll scream until you can scream no more!" She offers this advice: "If you scare easily, maybe you shouldn't go on."

Dawna calls this "the scariest show I've ever seen. It feels like the alien is right behind you."

The Timekeeper

Travel through time with Timekeeper, an Audio-Animatronics robot who's your host for this attraction. With his assistant, 9-Eye, Timekeeper takes you on a tour of the past and the future. You experience the ice age and see the creation of the Eiffel Tower. You meet a talented young musician named Mozart. You even get to spend time with Jules Verne and H.G. Wells, two of the first science-fiction writers.

9-Eye is a female droid whose oversize head is filled with nine cameras. She travels from century to century, sending back pictures that fill the nine screens of the Circle-Vision 360 theater. The movie makes it seem as if you're moving through time with her.

"This made me dizzy but still is sort of neat," says Lindsay. "I felt like it was more than just a movie." Dawna agrees. "I felt as if I was actually moving," she says. "This is a very funny show. If there's a long line, it would definitely be worth the wait."

Tate also really enjoys this. He likes that Timekeeper is played by the very funny actor Robin Williams. (The other stars in the show are Rhea Perlman, Jeremy Irons, and Michel Piccoli). Tate says, "The antics of Robin Williams make this attraction what it is." Karyn also likes Robin Williams. "But I don't think I would wait in a long line for it. If I had time and there wasn't a crowd, I'd go on it," she says.

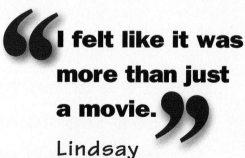

"I felt like it was more than just a movie."

Lindsay (age 9)

Carousel of Progress

An Audio-Animatronics family stars in scenes that show how electricity has improved American life. This exhibit made its debut at the New York World's Fair in 1964. There's now another scene at the end predicting how the family might live in the year 2000.

The show is called Carousel of Progress because you travel around the scenes in a circle, just like on a carousel. Sometimes it's hard to tell if it's the stage or the audience that's moving.

Most of the kids enjoy this show. "I really appreciate the story," says Tate. "It's a down-to-earth look at how the American family has progressed over the years."

Anna finds it "a good way to learn. I think it's cool when they say, in the early scenes, how 'that will never happen,' and we know that it already has."

Adam W. likes "how we learn about all the inventions that were created in the years past."

Danielle notices that "the sets look very realistic. It's interesting going through history that way." Brad's favorite is "the part at the end when the Granny is playing the virtual-reality game. It's neat how they go from year to year, but the last scene is the best."

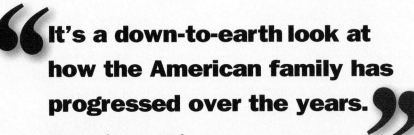

It's a down-to-earth look at how the American family has progressed over the years.

Tate (age 13)

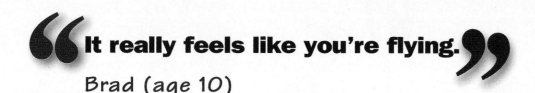

"It really feels like you're flying."

Brad (age 10)

Take Flight

Trace the history of aviation on a journey that takes you from man's first attempts at flight through the many advances in technology. The start of the trip features a giant pop-up book to show you that the story of flight is about to unfold. As you ride along, you see two movie sequences that make you feel like you're part of the action.

You also see a full-size section of the first type of airplane to cross the Atlantic Ocean. Notice how luxurious travel was in those days. Look at the scenes of foreign places that planes make it possible to visit.

Near the end of the ride, you pass through a jet engine. Special effects re-create the engine's rotation and make you feel like you're spinning. The last scene is another pop-up book showing London and New York.

The kids enjoy parts of this ride, but think it needs a narrator. "An announcer to explain all the things you're seeing would be good," says Taran. "This is a learning ride, so they should teach more."

The kids give high marks to the movie sequence that makes you feel like you're flying, and to the spinning engine. Brad says, "When you're supposed to be in the airplane, it really feels like you're flying." Robert agrees. "When you're watching the movie, it's like you're actually there," he says. "I like the big pop-up books, too."

Lindsay says, "I thought we would take off and go fast. But it's really slow." Danielle thinks that's the way it should be. "Then you can watch all the scenery," she says.

For Brian L., the ride gets better as it goes along. "When it first starts, it goes so slowly. But then it feels like you're flying and going much faster than you really are. That's pretty neat," he says.

All the kids agree with Anna: "If there is a line, don't wait. But if you have the time, it's okay."

Tomorrowland Speedway

Y ou can drive your own car (as long as you're 52 inches tall) on a lap around the racetrack at the Grand Prix. The cars travel along a track, but it's not as easy as it looks. Even expert drivers have some trouble. The cars are real and are powered by gasoline. They have rack-and-pinion steering and disc brakes, and travel at about seven miles per hour.

"No matter how perfectly you drive, it always goes off the track," says Nita. Brian L. agrees. "It feels like you don't have very good control of the car and you don't go very fast," he says.

Some of the kids really enjoy driving their own cars. "I love it. I think it goes pretty fast and I like having my own car," says Robert. Ashley P. agrees. "It's fun driving

my own car. But they should have it without the track."

David and Karyn think the ride gets boring once you've done it a few times. "I like the ride, but I wish they didn't have the track in the middle. It gets a little boring after a while," says David.

Karyn agrees. "It used to be one of my favorites, but it's a little boring now," she says. "I don't think very young kids would like it because they can't drive, and that's the whole fun of it."

Astro Orbiter

At the center of Tomorrowland is Rockettower Plaza—a tower that glows with colorful flashing lights. At the top is Astro Orbiter, a ride with giant, spinning rockets. They take you past whirling planets and give you a great view of Tomorrowland.

"This is one of the few rides that everyone will really enjoy," says Tate. "It's fast, but not to the point that it's too scary." Dawna agrees. "It's a good ride for little kids because you can control whether your ship goes up or down," she says. "People who don't have the stomach for Space Mountain can go here because it still has the space theme." Lindsay likes "that you get to go up in an elevator to take the ride. When you go up high in your rocket, you get a pretty good view."

But to Karyn, "It's just like rides at the fair or at any other theme park. I think this is more for younger kids."

The **Tomorrowland Transit Authority** travels alongside or through most of the land's attractions. If you're not sure about going on Space Mountain, the view from here can help you decide. It's also interesting to note that the ride runs on a motor with no moving parts. That means it doesn't give off any pollution. "If people want to get off their feet, this is the place to be," says Dawna. "It's somewhat entertaining and relaxing. And you can see a lot of Tomorrowland in a very short time."

If you're just dying to ride the **Skyway** cable cars that travel between Tomorrowland and Fantasyland, this is the best place to board. The lines at the Tomorrowland station are much shorter, so get on here.

Attraction Ratings

YAWN
(Save for Last)

AWESOME
(See at Least Twice)

REALLY COOL
(Don't Miss)

COOL
(Check It Out)

- Space Mountain
- Splash Mountain
- Big Thunder Mountain Railroad
- The Haunted Mansion
- Legend of The Lion King
- Alien Encounter

- Peter Pan's Flight
- Mickey's Toontown Fair
- Pirates of the Caribbean
- Astro Orbiter
- Carousel of Progress
- Tomorrowland Speedway

- It's A Small World
- Jungle Cruise
- Swiss Family Treehouse
- Mad Tea Party
- Mr. Toad's Wild Ride
- Cinderella's Golden Carrousel
- The Hall of Presidents
- Dumbo, the Flying Elephant
- Skyway
- The Timekeeper
- Tomorrowland Transit Authority

- Walt Disney World Railroad
- Country Bear Jamboree
- Snow White's Adventures
- Take Flight
- Main Street Cinema
- Tropical Serenade
- Tom Sawyer Island
- Liberty Square Riverboat

My visit to the Magic Kingdom will include...

Epcot

Epcot, which stands for "Experimental Prototype Community of Tomorrow," is divided into two sections: Future World and World Showcase. On one side of the park, there is a very large lake known as World Showcase Lagoon.

When you first enter Epcot, you are in Future World. The pavilions here have exhibits and rides that explore communications, energy, imagination, the ocean, agriculture, and health. These topics may sound a little dull, but with just a few exceptions, the kids really enjoy the attractions here.

World Showcase is a group of miniature countries—Canada, the United Kingdom, France, Morocco, Japan, the United States, Italy, Germany, China, Norway, and Mexico—all arranged around the lagoon. Each Epcot country has copies of famous landmarks to make you feel as if you're visiting the real place.

There are a few movies to see, plus rides through Norway and Mexico. But mostly, World Showcase is designed to give you the flavor of the different cultures. Most of the people who work at the pavilions and in the restaurants and shops are actually from the represented countries.

Future World

Although Future World seems like it's just educational, there's a lot for kids to explore. Start out at Test Track, which opens in spring 1997. Then go to the Wonders of Life pavilion, and Honey, I Shrunk the Audience at Journey Into Imagination. Be sure to check out all of the hands-on activities at Innoventions, Wonders of Life, The Living Seas, and Journey Into Imagination. Save the rest of Future World for the afternoon, when it's less crowded.

INNOVENTIONS

Here's your chance to try out games, computers, the Internet, virtual reality, and other inventions, many of them so new they're not yet for sale in any store. You see the latest appliances and electronics from some of the world's best-known companies.

Innoventions is located in two huge buildings, each with different things to see. Sega, IBM, AT&T, General Electric, Apple, Family PC, General Motors, and many others have things to share and show. Best of all, these aren't just ideas or things that might happen. Some of the products are available right now, while others will be on the market during the next couple of years.

"This is one of the coolest places for kids," says Tate. "You should schedule at least a couple of hours to get the full effect." Ashley J. adds, "Time sure flies here!"

Interesting inventions are brought in every three months to

"It's neat because it has a lot of automatic stuff. "

Emma (age 9)

keep up with the newest ideas. That means the exhibits may be different during your visit. But no matter when you come, you'll get a taste of the future. As Ashley J. puts it, "The place changes all the time, so you can come again and again."

Karyn tried a virtual guitar that makes anyone sound like a musician. Brian F. and Ashley J. played a game that seemed to place them underwater, avoiding sharks and capturing treasure chests. When they moved, their images on the screen swam in the same direction.

Adam F. says, "I wanted to try virtual reality, but the exhibits were too crowded." Instead, he tested some of the computers. "One had this program where what you say comes up on the screen," he says. Emma tried a computer coloring book. "If you touch a color it will start drawing in that color," she says.

Brian F. is amazed by the video games. "There are so many, and they're all free," he says. His favorite thing "is getting to be on the Jay Leno show. Everyone can see you on the TV talking to him."

Dawna likes the house of the future, with its appliances to make

home life easier. "The inventors figured out how we can use a remote to open windows and even prepare breakfast," she says. "You could be miles away from home and turn on the oven." Emma adds, "It's neat because it has a lot of automatic stuff that can turn out the lights, water the plants, or do laundry."

There's lots more to do and see at Innoventions. If you're not sure where to start, try the show starring Bill Nye, the Science Guy. He tells you what to expect here and explains the creative process behind many of the inventions. Most of the kids find the movie a little boring, but admit it's a good way to learn what Innoventions has to offer.

Spaceship Earth

The symbol of Epcot is the giant silver ball that you can see from almost anywhere in the park. Inside the ball is the Spaceship Earth Ride, a journey that takes you through the history of communications. You travel in a "time machine" from the days of Cro-Magnon man (30,000 to 40,000 years ago) to the future. The highlight of the trip comes when your time machine reaches the top of the dome and you're in the middle of the communications revolution. There are some great special effects, including colorful laser beams.

The older kids like this attraction more than the younger ones. Ashley P. remembers that she didn't like the ride when she was younger, but "now it's much more interesting to me."

"Being inside the ball is cool," says Karyn. "Knowing that during the whole ride you're actually inside the huge thing you see outside is amazing."

Nita says, "The details are great, like the monk who is snoring. I especially love the Greek scene."

The details make the ride a lot more interesting. Look at the real hieroglyphics in the Egyptian scene. Notice, in the scene with the printing press, that the keys really work. Also, watch Michelangelo's arm as he paints the ceiling of the Sistine Chapel.

If you've been on this ride before, you may be in for a surprise. It was updated in 1995, and the newest scenes are a big hit with the kids. "They show how one day we'll be able to use virtual reality for a field trip instead of actually going to a certain place," Dawna says. Karyn also likes taking a look at the future. "My favorite part is the video phones," she says. "I really like all the changes. They make the ride a little more exciting."

After the ride, check out the AT&T Global Neighborhood exhibit. It offers lots of fun, hands-on ways to learn more about communications networks.

Don't go to Spaceship Earth first thing in the morning because that's when it's most crowded.

THE LIVING SEAS

Explore the deep waters of the Caribbean Sea in the world's largest aquarium. There are more than 5,000 sea creatures here, including sharks, dolphins, barracuda, sea lions, angelfish, and many more. Your sea exploration begins in the waiting area, where there are samples of old wet suits worn by the first divers. Then you see a video presentation and a movie. Next, you get on board a "hydrolator" to go down to explore the coral reef. Ask your parents if the hydrolator takes them deep underwater. Then tell them they've actually traveled less than an inch.

After a ride through the aquarium, you are left off at Sea Base Alpha. This is your chance to take a closer look at the creatures of the sea and to try out the many hands-on exhibits.

"Living Seas is really cool," says Robert. "I thought my ears popped in the hydrolator. It feels like you're going way down to the bottom of the sea, even though you're only going down three-quarters of an inch."

David says, "It's fun learning about the different kinds of fish in the ocean."

Brian L. likes the hands-on exhibits. "You can put your arms in a diving suit and try to move like you're in the ocean," he says.

Nita and Taran tried the diving suit test together. "We didn't pass," Nita says. "It's really difficult to do things in a suit like that. It shows how hard it is for real divers." Taran explains, "I reached out and pulled the lever, but nothing happened. It's really hard."

Karyn "just loves the manatees. The rest of the exhibits are okay," she says, "but I prefer to see the real animals."

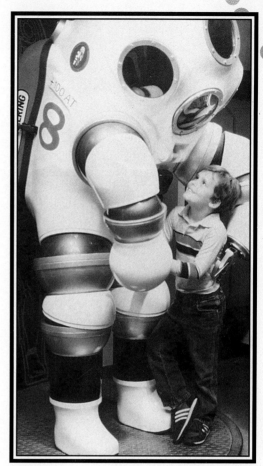

Taran and Robert agree. "The manatees are really cool," Taran says. And Robert adds, "I saw a spotted eagle ray, which is like a stingray. That was cool, too."

"It feels like you're going way down to the bottom of the sea.

Robert (age 8)

THE LAND

This pavilion focuses on one of everybody's favorite subjects—food. There's a boat ride through a greenhouse, a funny show about food, special guided tours, plus a movie about the environment featuring Simba, Timon, and Pumbaa from *The Lion King*.

Living with the Land

Set out on a boat trip through a simulated rain forest, desert, and prairie. See experimental technology that's used to grow plants in different environments. There's a desert farm with a drip irrigation system and another area where scientists are experimenting to see if fish can be grown like farm products.

This boat ride scores high marks with some of the kids. "It teaches about all of the different land regions," says Dawna. Brian L. likes that "it shows how plants can grow in soils like desert sand."

Adam W. says, "It's a long ride, but very worthwhile. It's neat how you get to see growing plants in the greenhouses." Danielle agrees. "I don't eat meat, so I like seeing how the food I eat is grown."

Lindsay loves this ride. "The greenhouses are amazing," she says. Justin learned a lot on this boat trip. "Before, I just knew that you put a seed into the ground and it grows. On the ride I learned more detail than that." Anna did not like this as much, but says, "It does show us new ways to make the best of our earth."

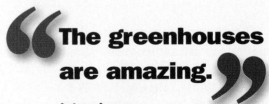

"The greenhouses are amazing."

Lindsay (age 9)

Food Rocks

Here's a rock concert with a lesson about good nutrition. Popular musicians, who have been turned into foods, perform favorite songs with new lyrics. Füd Wrapper, modeled after rap singer Tone Loc, is the host of this funny show. The introduction is a "heavy metal" song performed by four-foot-tall kitchen utensils.

Other performers include Chubby Cheddar, Neil Moussaka, Pita Gabriel, and The Refrigerator

Police, led by a milk carton wearing sunglasses.

In the pre-show area, there are murals with facts about food. Giant "smell boxes" can be found around the room. Open one and get a strong whiff of chocolate, garlic, coffee, bacon, orange, or seafood. Dawna points out the carpeting, with its pattern of forks, knives, and spoons.

The kids like the show, but think it's best for a younger audience. "This is a clever idea and a good way to teach kids about nutrition and the right foods to eat," says Lindsay. Tate calls Food Rocks "a cute show for little kids." Dawna likes "the Füd Wrapper and all of the other singers. I wouldn't go to this right before or after eating because it makes you feel guilty for eating food that's not good for you," she says.

Most of the kids like the names of the performers and the songs they sing. But sometimes it's hard to make out the lyrics. "I can't understand the words of the songs," Lindsay says. "I do think their names are clever, though."

Circle of Life

Simba, Timon, and Pumbaa are together again in this movie on protecting the environment. It mixes animation and live footage to show some of the problems we face—and how we can fix them.

The opening scene is filled with animals just like in *The Lion King*, but these animals are real. Next you see Simba near a watering hole. All of a sudden he hears "Timber!" and is drenched by the splash of a fallen tree. The woodcutters are Timon and Pumbaa, who are clearing the savanna to build the Hakuna Matata Lakeside Village.

Simba remembers what his father taught him about caring for the land. He tells his friends a story about a creature who sometimes forgets that everything is connected in the great Circle of Life. "That creature," Simba says, "is man."

Brian F. gets the message of this film. "It means to recycle, don't pollute, and don't litter," he explains. "I like the pictures they took of the fish, birds, alligators, penguins, and bears. And the cartoons are funny."

For Emma, "This movie is a nice reminder about what happens when we forget about the Circle of Life." Ashley J. takes the film to heart. "It really makes you want to change everything. I'm going to recycle more!" she says.

Greenhouse Tour

Kids (and parents) who are very interested in the environment can sign up for this one-hour guided tour of the growing areas at The Land pavilion. It costs $6 for adults and $4 for kids ages 3 to 9. You'll need reservations. Make them at the podium at the Green Thumb Emporium.

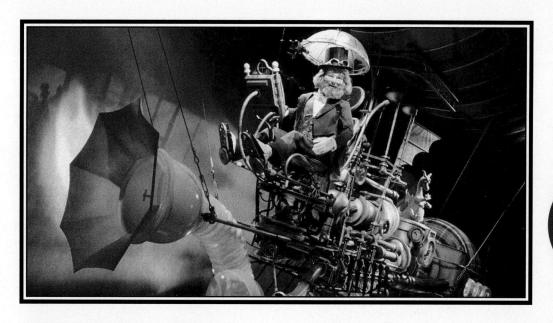

JOURNEY INTO IMAGINATION

Your host for this pavilion is Figment—a magical creature created from a lizard's body, a crocodile's nose, a steer's horns, two big yellow eyes, two small wings, and a pinch of childish delight. Figment is most often thought of as a baby dragon. He's so popular that he has become a mascot for Epcot.

Inside the pavilion is a ride through the wonders of the imagination, a hands-on activity center called Image Works, and a 3-D movie called Honey, I Shrunk the Audience. Outside the pavilion are the Leap Frog Fountains, whose streams of water leap from one garden to another in the most amazing way.

There are so many fun things to see and do in Image Works that the kids think you should plan on spending at least an hour at this pavilion.

"You keep seeing the dragon and what he's imagining."

Lindsay (age 9)

Journey Into Imagination Ride

Figment and his pal Dreamfinder lead you on a tour of the imagination. They show you how the five senses send messages to the brain to create dreams and ideas. This colorful ride is full of puffy clouds. It also has special effects like lasers and lightning.

About three-quarters of the way through the ride, you'll see a flash of light. Smile, because your picture is being taken. Look for it later, on a screen at the end of the ride.

"I like the little purple dragon," says Brad. "The ride is a little slow, but it's still cool."

Lindsay thinks the scenery is "very creative. You keep seeing the dragon and what he's imagining." Dawna agrees, saying, "The scenery is fantastic."

Anna's favorite part is that "they show you all the cool things you can do with art, like the sparkles, holograms, paints, and lights."

But Adam W. thinks the ride is too long. "I like the characters, but it's a little boring," he says. Tate agrees. "I think younger kids would like it best, though it does have a lot of neat stuff to look at."

> ## If you stand in the right place you can get totally wet.
>
> Taran (age 9)

Leap Frog Fountains

The arcing streams of water move from one garden plot to the next with no obvious pattern. That makes this area a highlight for kids of all ages.

"If you stand in the right place you can get totally wet," says Taran. "It's one of my favorite things." Robert agrees. "It's really cool and I like getting wet," he says.

Nita thinks it's neat "how the water jumps over your head." Brian F. has "never seen fountains do that before. They really do look like they're leaping over each other." Lissy likes how the fountains "keep you on your toes. If you're hot, you can just stand there and get a refreshing break."

Image Works

Once you get inside Image Works, it may be hard to leave. This is heaven for kids, with lots of hands-on (and feet-on) activities. The Rainbow Corridor is a tunnel full of neon tubes in all the colors of the rainbow. Walk through it and you'll reach Stepping Tones, where you step on colored lights on the floor to trigger different sounds. It's especially fun when you're with lots of people and everyone joins in. Other activities include Lumia, a seven-foot plastic ball that shows swirling lights and colors when different voices are heard. The Magic Palette has a special stylus and a touch-sensitive screen that let you create all kinds of images using bright colors. At the Electronic Philharmonic you can conduct an

"**They have everything a kid could need to occupy herself.**"

Lissy
(age 11)

orchestra by raising and lowering your hands.

"This place is totally awesome," says Lissy. "They have everything a kid could need to occupy herself."

Nita agrees. "There's so much to do. My favorite was directing the band." Ashley P. thinks "the lights and colors are cool, and it's neat how many things there are to do."

David likes "having all the hands-on experiences. It's a very fun place," he says.

Honey, I Shrunk the Audience

Inside the Imagination Theater is a movie based on *Honey, I Shrunk the Kids* and *Honey, I Blew Up the Kid*. This time, you're the one who gets shrunk, along with everyone else in the audience. Even the theater seems to shrink. You get attacked by 3-D mice, a 3-D lion, and a 3-D snake! Then the kid who was blown up in the movie picks up the theater and carries it around. Somehow you're brought back to your actual size, but only after some unusual adventures.

As Brian F. tells it, "First the professor shrinks himself. Then he accidentally hits the laser and shrinks us! The people on the screen are really big." Emma adds, "It makes you feel really small."

Dawna thinks "a lot of the 3-D looks like it's right in your face. I would recommend this if you liked the *Honey, I Shrunk the Kids* movie." Adam F. likes the 3-D effects more than any he's seen before. "They're more interactive," he says. "They do things to us instead of to other characters on the screen. When the boy picks us up, it feels like the theater moves."

Brian F. says, "When the 3-D mice come out, other effects somehow make it seem like the mice are really there. It's really cool." Ashley J. also finds the effects believable. "I even put my feet up!" she says.

"This is a very neat experience," says Lindsay. "Some parts might be scary for little kids because the characters come out so far."

Tate says, "This attraction really gives you the feeling that you're shrinking. There's a neat twist at the end." But we won't tell you what it is. As Emma puts it, "I don't want to give any more away. It's nice having a surprise."

Sketch Pad

TEST TRACK

Do you have what it takes to test drive a car? Find out in this thrilling new ride—and get an up-close look at what cars must go through to be safe.

Test Track is Walt Disney World's longest, fastest ride. You must be 40 inches tall to try it, and kids under 7 must be with an adult. Sporty test vehicles travel on a track that's almost a mile long. Your car has no steering wheel or brake pedals, but its audio and video equipment lets you know what's being tested.

You zip around curves, zoom down a straightaway, and ride on bumpy roads to see how your car handles different road conditions. Your car enters special hot and cold chambers to make sure it can stand up to the worst weather. The track also takes you outside the pavilion for the fastest part of the trip.

At one point, you hear the blast of a horn—just in time to avoid a crash with a big truck. Then your car heads straight toward a barrier.

Test Track is scheduled to open in May 1997. Until then, you can visit a preview center to get an idea of what to expect. That's what we did on our trip.

"I can't wait to go on this ride," says Adam F. "It will really let us know how they test cars because it puts you in the place of the test driver." Emma adds, "The cars get hot and cold, go slow and fast, and almost crash—just like test cars."

Ashley J. thinks the ride sounds "fast and fun. Everyone will like it." But younger kids might feel more like Brian F. "I don't think I would go on because it looks scary," he says.

Don't worry—it's safer than it looks. After all, that's what test driving is all about.

I like learning about everyone's hopes for the future.

David (age 13)

HORIZONS

Experience life in the future as you make your way through scenes showing a typical family in different environments. In the first scene, transportation and communication systems—such as holographic telephones and magnetic-levitation trains—help keep faraway family members close. The second scene shows robots harvesting fruits and vegetables that have been grown in a desert. The third scene takes place in a floating city, where schoolchildren take underwater field trips. The last setting is outer space, where family members stay in shape by playing games like zero-gravity basketball.

What happens at the end of the ride is up to you and the three other people in your car. Majority rules as you choose from land, sea, or space. Your car tilts back and vibrates, and special sound effects and close-up film sequences make you feel like you're moving very fast.

"I like the part where you choose where you want to go," says Nita. "It should be longer, though, because it's very interesting."

Ashley P. says, "In the underwater part, it's cool how everyone is eating. I like that they show you how they think the future will be."

Robert likes that the cars turn sideways "so you can really see everything."

David thinks there's a lot to see along the way. "There are many details, like the scuba class going by in the beginning, which you see again later on," he says. "I like learning about everyone's hopes for the future."

WONDERS OF LIFE

This pavilion has the kids' two favorite Epcot attractions— Body Wars, the exciting ride through the human body, and Cranium Command, a great show about how the brain works. There are also many hands-on activities, *The Making of Me* (a movie about the birth of a baby), a cartoon show about health that stars Goofy, and much, much more. It's easy to spend a couple of hours here, so come early to beat the crowds.

Body Wars

Fasten your seat belt for a rough ride through the human body. You must be at least 40 inches tall to ride. It all takes place on a flight simulator like the ones used to train astronauts and pilots. Before entering, you're miniaturized for a special rescue mission to help a scientist who gets stuck while trying to remove a splinter. Together, the simulator and the movie on the screen make you feel like you're really inside the body. The same technology is used at Star Tours at the Disney-MGM Studios, but Body Wars is a rougher ride.

Karyn says, "I like all the special effects, but it's too bumpy." Brian L. feels the same way. "You really get jerked around too much, and I don't like that kind of ride," he says.

The ride is still a favorite for most of the kids. "I love it," says Robert. "It's not scary at all, and it's cool and fun the way you go through the body." Ashley P. agrees. "I really like bumpy rides, so I like this one a lot."

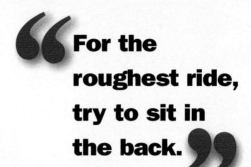
Cranium Command

Imagine that you're a pilot. But instead of flying an airplane, you pilot the brain of a 12-year-old boy. That's what happens to Buzzy in this attraction. The first part of the show takes place outside the theater, in a preview area. There you see a funny animated movie that explains how Buzzy gets his job. Then you go into the theater—and inside the brain with Buzzy. You watch as he tries to get all the parts of the brain to work together.

"You think it will be a little story about the brain or something," says Taran. "Instead it turns out to be a really cool thing."

Lissy agrees. "I like it because you learn different things about the brain and how it works with the rest of your body—and you have a lot of fun at the same time." And Karyn thinks that "it's very educational as well as cute and funny."

Nita has been on it a few times "and I still like it. For the roughest ride, try to sit in the back," she advises.

"You really have to hold on to the arms of the seats or you get thrashed around," warns Taran. "I think it should take longer to get from the heart to the brain, or that you should go all the way down to the feet and then bounce up to the brain," he adds.

If some people in your group don't want to go on Body Wars, there's plenty for them to do at Wonders of Life. And you can meet them when you get off the ride.

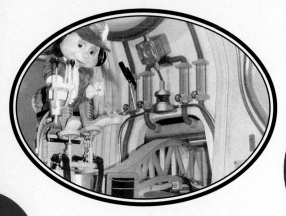

Hot Tip
Pay attention to the pre-show.

Be sure to pay attention to that first movie. Dawna says, "I like the funny film at the beginning. It explains what will happen in the theater." Robert adds, "If you don't see the pre-show, you'll go crazy trying to figure out what's going on."

The brain in Cranium Command belongs to a boy named Bobby. Once inside the brain, you see Buzzy trying to pilot Bobby through a day at school. "It's very comical," Tate says. "I really can relate to some of the things that happen to the boy in the story because he's about my age." Anna says, "I recommend this to all ages, especially teenagers."

Brad likes how the parts of the brain each are played by a different character. "I like all the stars, like the guy in the stomach from 'Cheers,' and Hans and Franz pumping the heart." He notices that "the left brain would always make things realistic." Robert adds that "the left brain is totally logical and the right brain is crazy."

Lindsay advises that you pay attention. "I didn't know what to look at first. There's so much going on." All the details make this a show you can enjoy more than once.

The show helped all the kids understand how the brain works. Lindsay says, "This is funny and a perfect way to learn about your body." Besides, as Brian L. points out, "It's a lot of fun to see all the different things that go on in our brain each day."

The kids agree that Cranium Command is one attraction that's kind of hidden in the Wonders of Life pavilion. None of them had ever seen it—even though some had been to the World before. So don't miss it!

Fitness Fairgrounds

The lobby of the Wonders of Life pavilion has so many hands-on activities, the kids think you can spend at least an hour here. The Wonder Cycles are computerized bicycles that let you watch film footage while riding. In the Coach's Corner, tennis, baseball, and golf swings are analyzed, and you get tips for a better game. The Sensory Funhouse has many different hands-on choices. The kids enjoy trying to guess what certain objects are without being able to see them.

"There's tons of stuff to do," says Dawna. "I like the bicycles. At the end it tells you how many miles you've gone."

Adam W. made a good showing at the Coach's Corner. "I really like the baseball critique. It's neat how they can tell you what you're doing wrong," he says.

Justin likes that "you can touch everything. It's so much fun." Lindsay agrees. "It's really fun and different from other places."

Anna likes "how you can experiment hands-on, and you can figure things out for yourself. With the bright colors and decorations, this is the perfect Walt Disney World attraction."

There are many other activities at the Wonders of Life pavilion. **Goofy About Health** is a cartoon show about how Goofy goes from being a sloppy-living guy to a health-conscious fellow. At the **AnaComical Players Theater**, you see a corny but informative show about good health. *The Making of Me* is a movie about the birth of a baby that shows real scenes in a hospital. A must.

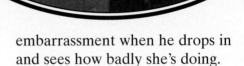

UNIVERSE OF ENERGY

This pavilion looks at the many ways in which energy was originally created—and how it's created today. The show includes three films and a ride through prehistoric times, complete with huge dinosaurs. The attraction was recently spruced up, and is a lot more fun than before.

The show starts with a movie about Ellen, a woman who's watching a TV game show. Her friend, Judy, is on the show, doing great. Ellen is playing along at home and striking out, especially in the "Energy" category. Even worse, her neighbor is Bill Nye, the Science Guy. Imagine her

embarrassment when he drops in and sees how badly she's doing.

Bill leaves and poor Ellen needs a nap. She dreams she's on the game show, playing against Judy and Albert Einstein. Ellen scores less than zero and wakes up in a sweat. Luckily, Bill Nye comes to the rescue to teach Ellen about energy.

Next, the theater separates into several sections, taking you and Ellen on a ride to a prehistoric world. You travel through fog, and past huge trees, real-looking lava, and several types of dinosaurs, including a brontosaurus, an allosaurus, an elasmosaurus, and pteranodons. These are some of the largest animals like this ever made.

Then it's on to another theater, with a short film on civilization and possible sources of energy. At the end, Ellen's dreams give her one more shot at the TV game show. How does she do? That's something you'll see for yourself!

notes

World Showcase

Touring the World Showcase pavilions, with all the different shops, attractions, and entertainment, is interesting to kids. But most agree that they would like more things geared to them. Dawna points out that "the pavilions with a ride or movie are more fun. I'd also like to talk more to the people who work there about their countries." Lindsay wanted to take a guided tour. "A tour guide could tell you all about the countries. Each one has lots of details, and some of them make you feel like you're really there," she says.

CANADA

The beauty of America's northern neighbor is on display at this pavilion. There's a rocky mountain, a rushing stream, beautiful gardens, and a totem pole. The highlight at the Canada pavilion is a movie called *O Canada!* It was filmed using a technology called Circle-Vision 360, so the Canadian scenery surrounds you completely. The theater has no seats. You stand, so it's easy to turn around and see the whole picture.

The movie takes a coast-to-coast look at Canada, including scenes of skiers, dogsledders, and ice skaters in the snowy Canadian Rockies. Eagles, bobcats, wolves, bears, deer, bison, and herds of reindeer all were filmed in their natural settings. Cities and towns are part of the film, too. You can also see covered bridges, sailing ships, and even the Royal Canadian Mounted Police.

"The movie is pretty and there are many beautiful scenes," says Nita. "But I don't like standing up. They need seats in that theater!"

"All the mountains and sledding scenes are beautiful."
Karyn (age 13)

Ashley P. likes how much she learned about Canada. "I like the music and I like all the information the movie gives you about Canada," she says. "The winter scenes are my favorites."

Karyn agrees. "All the mountains and sledding scenes are beautiful," she says.

The Circle-Vision 360 technique makes you feel like you're actually part of the movie. David explains, "I think it's neat how Circle-Vision makes you feel like you're moving. Plus the movie shows a lot of the culture of Canada, and I like seeing all the buildings and rivers."

Brian L. agrees. "I like how they make you feel like you're moving," he says. "I think it's great—I like every part of the film."

Lissy thinks the movie has a few boring spots, but "they explain Canada well. There should be more moving sensations, though."

UNITED KINGDOM

From London to the English countryside, this pavilion gives a varied view of the United Kingdom. Some details worth looking for include the smoke stains painted on the chimneys to make them look old, and the thatched roofs that are really made of plastic broom bristles. And Tate points out, "If you like flowers, there are pretty gardens here." There's not much to do but look in the shops. Lindsay likes "looking at the different stores from the outside." Also, a group of comedians often performs along World Showcase Promenade near this pavilion.

FRANCE

The Eiffel Tower is the most recognizable landmark at the France pavilion. But it's not as tall as it seems. The same technique that makes Cinderella Castle appear taller than it is—forced perspective—is used here to make the Eiffel Tower seem to loom over Paris. The buildings are designed to look just like those you would see in a French town. Many of the people who work at the pavilion are French and speak English with a French accent.

The main attraction at the France pavilion—aside from the delicious treats at the bakery—is *Impressions de France* (Impressions of France), an 18-minute movie that takes you from one end of France to the other. The movie is shown on a 200-degree screen, so you get to sit down and take in all the beautiful views. There are village scenes with flower markets, pastry shops, and lovely homes. There are shots of the real Eiffel Tower, the Palace of Versailles, the French countryside, wine and champagne vineyards, the Alps, the French Riviera, and much more.

Even though it's not a Circle-Vision 360 movie, it really feels as if you're moving—especially the skiing in the Alps scene. The music is the perfect sound track for the movie. Most of it is by French composers.

"This movie makes me want to go to France," says Taran, "especially for the skiing." Anna agrees. "Now I'd like to go see all those places. I also love the music," she says.

Karyn has been to France, and she recognizes many of the places. "It's very interesting to me because

66 This movie makes me want to go to France. 99

Taran (age 9)

I've been to a lot of parts of France. I think it's more fun if you know what you're looking at."

Ashley P. is less enthusiastic. "It doesn't give enough information about France." Danielle thinks "they should explain more. But I do like the pictures they show because France is a beautiful place."

Lissy thinks "the pictures describe themselves. I also like when you feel like you're moving," she says. Brad especially likes "the flying parts. It feels like you're really there."

Robert says, "This is my favorite of the movies at Epcot. I like that you can sit down and rest your legs." Brian L. thinks the "music is great, and I like the skiing and what they show of the country." Lindsay sums it up: "This movie has colorful pictures and is a great way to learn about France."

MOROCCO

Nine tons of handmade tile were shipped to Epcot to build the Moroccan pavilion. Moroccan artists also were brought in to make sure the mosaics or tilework would be authentic. There are replicas of monuments from several cities, including Marrakesh and Fez. A working waterwheel takes care of the irrigation for the gardens around the pavilion. There are lots of shops selling the types of things you would find in Morocco. You can buy handcrafted rugs, baskets, brass, jewelry, or a fez and other traditional Moroccan clothing. There's also a shop with *Aladdin* merchandise. The restaurant here has a belly dancer who entertains in the courtyard, too.

Don't miss the entertainment at each of the countries.

JAPAN

The pagoda out front makes the Japanese pavilion easy to spot. It's modeled after a pagoda in the city of Nara. The landscaping was done according to the strict Japanese method of garden design. Notice all of the evergreen trees, which in Japan are symbols of eternal life. Some of the trees found in a traditional Japanese garden will not survive in Orlando, so similar trees were used as substitutes. A drum-playing duo often performs outside the pavilion. It's also fun to watch the stilt walkers that look like birds. The Mitsukoshi Department Store is huge and has lots of reasonably priced souvenirs from Japan.

THE AMERICAN ADVENTURE

This pavilion is the centerpiece of World Showcase. The building was constructed with 110,000 bricks—each made by hand. The American Adventure show inside celebrates the American spirit from the earliest days right up to the present. The show is narrated by Audio-Animatronics figures of Benjamin Franklin and Mark Twain. These two figures were made with the latest technology, so it's hard to tell they aren't real.

The show pays tribute to many of the heroes of our country: the Pilgrims, Alexander Graham Bell,

"It's neat to see all the historic figures."

Brad
(age 10)

Charles Lindbergh, Jackie Robinson, Walt Disney, and many more. Historic events are shown on large screens behind the characters. The show also includes events that have taken place during the last ten years.

The kids enjoy this show but think it needs more narration. Dawna says, "It's great, but for kids who haven't studied a lot of history yet, we don't understand every scene." Brad agrees. "I don't understand a lot of it, but the people look so real. It's neat to see all the historic figures."

Adam W. says, "The characters are so realistic. I like how they walk and all the detail on their faces." Tate thinks the show is "very descriptive and very real."

Justin wasn't sure at first if the characters are actors or Audio-Animatronics. "I was confused. I couldn't tell if they're real."

Anna thinks this show is "the perfect way to learn about our heritage. The best part is the movie at the end, which reviews all the famous Americans."

ITALY

Venice, the Italian city known for its canals, is the inspiration for this pavilion. The tower is a smaller version of the Campanile in Venice. The main building was designed to look like the Doge's Palace. Be sure to notice the gondolas tied to the dock in World Showcase Lagoon.

Look for The Living Statues in

the courtyard. They stand perfectly still, and then move when you least expect it. An open-air market has tasty Italian chocolates and other goodies for sale. The specialty at the restaurant here is fettucine Alfredo. The waiters and waitresses sing, which Anna says "really adds to the atmosphere. It feels like you're in Italy."

GERMANY

There isn't a village in Germany quite like the one at Epcot. Instead, it's a combination of cities and small towns from all around the country. They are blended together to offer

a German flavor. Try to stop by for a visit at the top of any hour so you can see and hear the specially designed glockenspiel chime.

Danielle says, "The buildings in Germany look authentic. In the center is a beautiful statue on top of a waterfall. I also like the cobblestone pavement." Tate suggests you "try the soft pretzels sold here. There's not much else to do, but it's cool to see how the buildings look in Germany."

CHINA

At the center of this pavilion is the Disney version of the Temple of Heaven, a landmark in the Chinese city of Beijing. Acrobats perform in the courtyard and music adds to the overall atmosphere.

Inside the Temple of Heaven is another Circle-Vision 360 movie called *Wonders of China: Land of Beauty, Land of Time.* Before going in to see the movie, take a look at the waiting area. It's decorated in red and gold, and features exhibits on Chinese art and culture. When we were there, the exhibit was all

"The dragon stuff is really cool."

Robert (age 8)

about dragons. It may be different for your visit.

Wonders of China is a stand-up movie like *O Canada!* The 19-minute film shows a view of China that many people—kids and grownups—have never seen. The Chinese cities and countryside, its people, and all their ancient traditions are depicted. It's a beautiful movie, but one that's appreciated more by adults and by kids who have studied China.

"I think it's pretty interesting, but that's because I just finished studying China a few weeks ago in school," says Nita.

Karyn prefers the waiting area. "The exhibit is cool and the marble benches are pretty," she says. "I think the movie is boring. I'm not really that interested in China."

Robert, who knows a lot about dragons, likes the waiting area. "The dragon stuff is really cool. They have some neat things in there, and since I love dragons, this was my favorite part," he says. "I think the movie is boring."

Most of the kids agree that the movie is better for their parents and other adults. "It's really boring—a complete yawn," says David. Lissy agrees. "I just don't think it's very interesting," she says.

NORWAY

The history, folklore, and culture of one of the world's oldest countries are the focus of this pavilion. The central building is a Norwegian castle, modeled after an ancient fortress that still stands in the capital city of Oslo. Inside is the Maelstrom ride through Norwegian history. You board dragon-headed

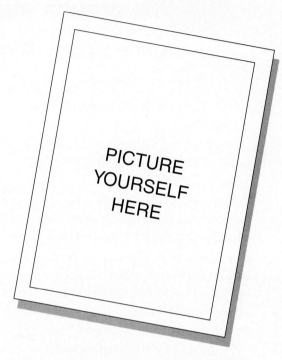

PICTURE
YOURSELF
HERE

Viking boats like the one that Eric the Red sailed in.

The ride begins in a Viking village, where a ship is being built to go out to sea. The next scene takes place in the forest, where a three-headed troll curses your boat and causes it to start backing up. You are heading for a waterfall and the boat seems as if it will go over backwards. Then, just in time, it

moves forward again. The ride has a few more unexpected dips and turns, and there are lightning flashes and other special effects.

After leaving the boat, you see a movie about Norway that helps explain some of the history and folklore you see on the boat ride.

Dawna says, "I like how we sit in a boat just like the ones from Norway." Brad likes how "at first you think you're going down the waterfall backward." Lindsay agrees. "It's really unpredictable. You think you're going to drop, and then you get turned back."

The kids agree that the scenery is confusing if you don't know much

"At first you think you're going down the waterfall backward. "

Brad (age 10)

about Norway. "I think the movie should be first so you'll know what you're looking at on the ride," says Karyn. But Danielle has read a book about the legends of Norway, "so it's really interesting when you see them," she says. Tate adds, "The video we saw was very entertaining while it taught us about their history."

David wishes the ride was longer. "But I still think it's the best thing in World Showcase, even though it's so short."

MEXICO

The pyramid-shaped building at the Mexico pavilion is home to El Río del Tiempo: The River of Time. This is a slow boat trip through scenes of Mexican life. You see Mexico in past centuries as well as in modern times. Film clips show cliff divers in Acapulco, speed boats in Manzanillo, and beautiful sea creatures in Isla Mujeres. There are many colorful displays depicting Mexican traditions. At the end of the boat ride, you can visit several shops with Mexican crafts,

sombreros, and colorful blankets.

Brad thinks "the boat ride is neat. There are so many things to look at." Anna agrees. "It's a good thing the boat goes slowly, so you can see all the neat scenes and Mexican figurines," she says. "I like how they have all the rocks and the atmosphere of different parts of Mexico."

For Dawna, the art is the most interesting part. "I like all the paintings, because I think Mexican art is really neat." Adam W. agrees. "I love the detail of the paintings," he says. Tate likes the way "the ride shows the beauty of the country."

89

Attraction Ratings

AWESOME
(See at Least Twice)

REALLY COOL
(Don't Miss)

COOL
(Check It Out)

YAWN
(Save for Last)

- Test Track (We just know it's going to be great!)
- Wonders of Life
- Innoventions
- Image Works
- Leap Frog Fountains
- Honey, I Shrunk the Audience

- The Living Seas
- Journey Into Imagination Ride
- The Land
- Horizons
- Norway
- France
- Mexico

- Spaceship Earth
- Canada (ages 12 and up)
- The American Adventure (ages 12 and up)
- Food Rocks
- Universe of Energy

- China
- Italy
- United Kingdom
- Germany
- Morocco
- Japan

My visit to Epcot will include...

Disney-MGM Studios

The Disney-MGM Studios lets you see some of the magic of making movies and television programs. There are attractions that take you behind the scenes to see how animated movies are made, how sound effects are created and edited into movies, how special effects are done, and how stunts are performed.

Other attractions include a great 3-D movie starring the Muppets, a rough ride through space on a flight simulator, a chance to star in famous television scenes, a show that takes you "Under the Sea" with The Little Mermaid, and the newest show, Disney's The Hunchback of Notre Dame—A Musical Adventure.

One of the best things about the Studios is that you can participate in a number of attractions. It's fun to be right in the middle of the action, so be sure to volunteer.

It's also interesting to realize that movies and television shows are actually filmed here. During your visit, you may get a peek at people working on the next Disney animated movie, or get to see a movie or television show in the making. Some attractions open in late morning and showtimes vary. Pick up a guidemap so you can plan your tour around the park without wasting any time.

The Twilight Zone Tower of Terror

Tower of Terror is the tallest attraction at Walt Disney World. For some kids, it's also the scariest. Disney Imagineers have said this ride has a "scream factor" of five. That means most guests scream five times! You must be at least 40 inches tall to ride.

Legend says that lightning once struck this old, run-down hotel. When you look at it from the front, you can see the part that came off. As you wait in line, you walk through different rooms, including the lobby, the library, and the boiler room. Everything is exactly as it was the night of the storm. "When lightning struck, everything just stopped," Tate explains. "You can see where the people were. There's a glass with lipstick on it, a card game that was going on, and somebody's belongings are at the front desk."

You'll have plenty of time to look around if the line is long. But as Dawna points out, "waiting just makes the suspense worse." Try to visit first thing in the morning before it gets too crowded.

The ride itself is an elevator where you're seated and strapped in. Before you get on, you have one last chance to change your mind. If you decide this ride's not for you, there's another elevator that will take you to the exit. Just remember: Once you get on the ride elevator, you can't get off.

Most of the kids were nervous, even Tate, who thinks it's scarier after you've been on a couple of times. Adam F. points out that "you don't see the people coming off like on other rides. There's another exit." Lindsay offers a warning: "Younger kids should know that about half the ride is in the dark."

Say "cheese" when the elevator stops at an open window. Your picture's being taken.

The ride takes you on a mini tour of the hotel, where you see many high-tech special effects. Ashley J. says, "There are surprises around every corner." Adam F. likes "the effects like the stars and the window coming toward you and cracking." Lindsay says, "I particularly like the ghosts of the people who disappeared."

Then there's a series of drops. The first is about eight stories. The elevator shoots back up quickly and you end up on the 13th floor of the hotel. There are lots of sound effects that make you think the cables are breaking. Next you plunge 13 stories. Suddenly, the elevator shoots up again. When it gets to the top, it barely stops before dropping to the ground a final time. This last part happens so quickly it feels a bit like a hill on a roller coaster.

The kids all agree that the ride is a scary one. Ashley J. says, "Waiting to fall is the scariest part." Emma adds, "It's good that there's more than one drop." Lindsay says, "It's a thrilling experience. I was flying out of my seat!"

Dawna agrees. "This ride is one of the scariest at Walt Disney World. You feel terrified before even falling. I was screaming all the way down." For Brian F., "It's spooky. There are all these noises. When you get to the top, the doors open and you look outside. It's really high, and then all of a sudden you go down really fast."

The drops are programmed by a computer, so the ride is different than when it first opened—and could change again. That's good news for Dawna, who "would definitely go on again." Tate says, "Everyone should go at least once."

Waiting to fall is the scariest part.
Ashley J. (age 12)

Indiana Jones Epic Stunt Spectacular

Fire, explosions, daring escapes, and other special effects are demonstrated at this highly rated attraction. Stunt men and women perform scenes from the movie *Raiders of the Lost Ark* and show how special effects are created. The audience watches from a large amphitheater, and several members are chosen (though no children are allowed) to perform with the pros.

"I love this show. I think it's great for all ages," says Karyn. Ashley P. agrees, "I think it's really neat how they do all the special effects, and how the fire blows up and how the tumblers tumble off the roofs."

One of the best parts of the show, according to all the kids, is the scene where the giant ball rolls down and seems to crush Indiana Jones. "I was at the edge of my seat!" says Brian L. Robert is amazed at the size of the ball. "The ball seems really heavy, so it would be so hard to get run over and stay alive," he says.

The kids also love the stunt men and women, and how they show us that dangerous movie stunts can be performed safely. "I love how they were falling from the towers, and then they were always okay—it's really neat," says Brian L.

Lissy says the music adds to the suspense and "the stunt people are just fantastic." Brian L. views it as pure excitement, "especially when three of them were jumping off the

trampoline and one landed in a really neat roll."

Not just entertaining, this is a show where you can learn a lot about movie stunts. "They really explain everything they're doing, making it even more fun to watch," says Karyn. David was on his feet the whole time. "It's fascinating seeing how they can get away with tricks like that," he says, "like how the guy went underground when we thought he was being chomped up by the fan."

Nita sums it up this way: "It's a show you can see many times and never get tired of it."

Star Tours

Soar into space on board an out-of-control StarSpeeder from the movie *Star Wars*. The flight is piloted by a new recruit, Captain Rex, who can't seem to find his way through all the giant ice crystals and the other spaceships. You must be at least 40 inches tall to ride.

This ride takes place on a flight simulator, the same type of device used to train astronauts and pilots. The combination of the simulator and the movie on the screen makes you feel like you're really rocketing through space.

Brad says, "The pilot makes the ride really fun. He keeps going the wrong way." Robert thinks "it's really neat. It's funny when the pilot can't find the brakes," he says. "If you know what the movie *Star Wars* is like, you'll really like this ride."

Danielle agrees. "It feels and looks like you're really traveling through space." Dawna adds, "It feels like you're going really fast even though you're not going anywhere." Anna likes "how the

---

Try to go to Star Tours first thing in the morning, but not right after breakfast.

seats move right to left, but the movie makes you feel like you're moving forward."

Some of the kids had been on Star Tours several times before. For them, this time wasn't as much fun. "After you go on it about ten times, it gets a little boring and seems short. But if you've never done it, it's a must," according to David. Ashley P. was on Star Tours for the second time. "It wasn't as much fun as the first," she says, "but I still like to get bumped around."

An experienced rider who's been on Star Tours about 15 times, Nita offers this advice: "If you're a person who likes a really rough ride, try to sit in the back."

Dawna would still go on it again and again. "It's one of the best rides at Walt Disney World," she says.

Jim Henson's Muppet* Vision 3–D

This is one of Walt Disney World's best attractions. It begins with a very funny pre-show starring Fozzie Bear, Gonzo, Scooter, and Sam Eagle. Then you go into a specially designed theater that looks just like the one from "The Muppet Show." You see incredible 3-D effects mixed with some live special effects—so it's hard to tell what's part of the movie and what's real. Most kids can't help reaching out at least once.

"The characters come right out at you," observes Lissy. "It's really cool that they have real things happening, so when they throw the pie you think it will be a real pie, too." Adam W. agrees. "My favorite parts are the squirting water and when the screen blows up, because it really happens. You feel like you're going to get hit."

The real bubbles are a great special effect. "You couldn't tell which were real and which were part of the movie," says Brian L. "It's really more like 4-D." Justin was also fooled by the special effect.

"When I tried to touch one of them, my hand reached right through."

Taran agrees. "The whole movie is in your face!" he says. "It's awesome. I also love the little 3-D spirit, Waldo, because he seems like he's talking only to you."

Robert and Anna feel the same way. "I thought the 3-D guy was just pointing at me. I can't believe he was pointing at everyone," says

"The whole movie is in your face!

Taran
(age 9)

Robert. And Anna says, "Waldo looks like he's always right in front of you."

Nita, Karyn, and Tate have seen this attraction before. Nita reminds you to look at the back of the theater from time to time "because there's a lot of stuff happening back there and most people miss it, at least on their first visit." Tate adds, "You can really enjoy this

attraction more than once."

Karyn says, "I just love this movie. You have to see it a few times to get all the jokes and appreciate more of the details, like the two guys sitting in the balcony. They're really funny."

SuperStar Television

This is your chance to star in a famous television show. Before going inside the theater, members of the audience are chosen to appear in scenes from shows such as "I Love Lucy," "Cheers," and "Home Improvement," or to hit a grand slam for the New York Mets. Some are chosen inside, too. There are a lot of people chosen, but they don't pick too many kids. If you think you'd like to be a star, be sure to stand in the front and wave and make lots of noise.

Once inside, the people picked from the audience act out scenes and their pictures are blended with the real programs. Don't worry if you're camera shy or don't get picked. Watching is just as much fun as being on screen.

"I think it's cool that they let you participate, but you don't have to if you don't want to," says Lissy.

Karyn was chosen to be a New York Mets baseball player. "I really liked being in it, but I wish I could have seen it, too," she says. Karyn got to hit a home run and then be interviewed by Howard Cosell.

100

Hot Tip
Stand in the front if you want to get picked for a part.

The rest of the kids enjoyed watching. "My favorite is the 'I Love Lucy' scene with the chocolates on the conveyor belt. It's fun to see people from the audience play the roles of famous actors," says Brian L.

"You can see it over and over again," says Nita, "because the

scenes are different depending on who gets picked. It can be really funny when people goof up."

Taran's favorite part "is the David Letterman scene when he drops things off the Empire State Building." David says, "The show is neat. I like how they have the characters in just the right parts so it looks real."

I really liked being in it, but I wish I could have seen it, too.

Karyn (age 13)

The Magic of Disney Animation

See how *Beauty and the Beast*, *Aladdin*, *The Lion King*, *Pocahontas*, *The Hunchback of Notre Dame*, and all the other Disney animated movies were created. And watch cartoon artists at work on future Disney hits, such as *Hercules* or *The Legend of Mulan*. A new highlight is the chance to meet and talk with a real Disney artist.

In the waiting area of this attraction, there are displays of "cels" from famous movies. (A cel is the actual painted film used in the animated movie.) There are also cels from movies that the animators are in the process of creating.

When it's time for the show, you go into a theater to see a very funny movie starring Robin Williams and Walter Cronkite. Robin is turned into a cartoon to teach us how animated films are

"It's fun but you can learn at the same time."

Lissy
(age 11)

made. After the movie, you can walk through the animation studio and see artists at work. To find out more about what they're doing, just look at the screens overhead. Robin Williams and Walter Cronkite star again. This time they're explaining each step of the animation process. Try to see this show during the day when the animators are busy working. They usually go home at about 5 P.M.

All the kids like the way this attraction makes learning fun. "I think Robin Williams is so funny," says Lissy. "It's fun but you can learn at the same time." Ashley P. agrees. "I like how they have Robin Williams as the character," she says. "And I like how much you learn about animation."

This attraction is especially interesting to Brian L., who has taken a class in cartoon drawing. "You can learn a lot by watching, and the movie is so funny," he says. "I like how you can see real cels."

David finds it "fascinating to see

all the cels that they really use in the movies. I love that you can walk through and see real animators at work. It's like taking your own personal tour."

Nita also likes the walking part of the tour the best. "It's so interesting just watching the artists work," she says. Karyn likes that they take you step-by-step through the animation process. "It's just so neat to see how they make animated movies," she says.

Honey, I Shrunk the Kids Movie Set Adventure

The backyard in this popular movie has been re-created as an oversize playground. Even grownups feel small here. There are 30-foot-tall blades of grass, giant tree stumps, huge LEGO toys, a big garden hose with a leak, and lots more. You have many places to explore and plenty of things to climb up and slide down.

"It looks more like 'Honey, I blew up the garden!'" says Taran. "I like the cave the best, but I advise you to take a friend because it's more fun with more people."

Robert likes it "because there are so many different places to go. This playground would never get boring for me."

Lissy thinks "the whole place is really neat. Not just the slides and the swings—there's a lot for older kids to notice, like all the things that look like they come straight from the movie."

The kids enjoy trying to get wet under the giant, leaky hose. This is a real challenge since water squirts

from a different spot each time.

Some of the older kids prefer watching the younger kids in action. "I like the slides and the big net, but I think it's more for younger kids," says Brian L.

Karyn agrees. "I'm the type of person who would just love to take a little kid around and watch them have fun."

Honey, I Shrunk the Kids Movie Set Adventure Checklist

- ☐ Bee Hive
- ☐ Cheerios
- ☐ Dog's Nose
- ☐ Leaky Hose
- ☐ Roll of Film Slide
- ☐ Spider Web
- ☐ Tree Slide
- ☐ Underground Cave

> ## "It's interesting to see all the old movies. "
>
> ### Ashley P. (age 11)

The Great Movie Ride

Take a ride through some of the most famous movies of all time. You pass through the sets from films including *Singin' in the Rain*, *The Wizard of Oz*, *Alien*, *Casablanca*, and *Mary Poppins*. You get caught in the middle of a shootout and come close to getting slimed by the alien. The ride ends with a movie that shows clips from great films.

"It's really cool, but it could have more action in it," says Robert. Brian L. thinks it's a little boring. "They tried to make it more exciting with the alien thing, but that isn't enough to make the ride really fun."

Karyn disagrees. "No matter how many times I ride, I still love it. I really love old movies, but if they want the ride to appeal to younger kids, Disney should update it so there are movies that kids know."

Ashley P. likes the ride just the way it is. "I think it's interesting to see all the old movies. I don't think

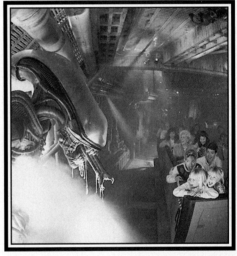

it should be more modern."

The kids agree that the guide plays a big role in how much they like the trip. "The first time I really liked it because the guide was good," says Taran. "The second time she wasn't as good, so it was a little boring."

Lissy says, "The ride explains the movies really well, and the characters look almost real. I like the songs, too."

Studio Backlot Tour

There's a real working studio at the Disney-MGM Studios. This tram ride takes you through parts of the backstage area where scenes from movies and television shows are filmed. Your trip includes Catastrophe Canyon—a great special effects show demonstrating an explosion, a fire, and a flash flood. And you see how a battle scene at sea is shot. You also get to see the costume department, the lighting department, and some props from famous movies.

The ocean battle scene is a favorite with Justin and Brad. "I really like the bombs in the water," says Justin. Brad likes "the torpedo in the beginning. I also like that we get to see how they do special effects, and then go where they actually make the films."

"You learn something the whole time while still having fun," says Lissy. "I really like Catastrophe Canyon. It shows that special effects are much safer than they look."

Robert agrees. "Catastrophe Canyon is really cool. When the explosions go off, it gets really hot.

If you like getting wet, sit on the left side of the tram.

Then when the water comes down, it gets really cold. I also like seeing the real airplane. The guide told us that it has been used in filming a lot of movies."

Brian L. thinks part of the tour is a little boring. "I love the Catastrophe Canyon part," he says, "but I'm not crazy about the rest."

Ashley P. enjoys touring the back streets where "seeing the houses without the backs is cool. They only shoot the front for the shows, so that's all they build," she points out.

"It's pretty cool how you get to see the actual homes from some television shows," adds David.

Taran is also interested in the back streets, but for a different reason. "Catastrophe Canyon is great, but I really like the movie props because I like building models," he says.

Nita has seen this attraction before. "I like this tour," she says, "but a lot depends on the guide. If you get a really good guide, the tour is much better."

D. DUCK

New York Street

In the back corner of the Disney-MGM Studios is a street that looks like it's part of Manhattan. You'll notice famous landmarks, including the Empire State Building and the Chrysler Building. The Empire State Building here is only four stories high, but seems as tall as the one in New York City.

Although they look pretty real, the skyscrapers are just painted flats. That means they have no backs. The other buildings are made mostly of fiberglass and Styrofoam. This street has to look true to life because film crews shoot movies here. Just ask Dawna, who's seen this street in a movie. "I thought the whole movie was filmed in New York," she says. "Then they show you all the sets here at the Studios."

Want to see something you won't find on the real streets of New York? Look for the lamppost with the umbrella. Pull the handle and it starts to rain on top of the umbrella. Ask your parents about the umbrella scene in the old movie *Singin' in the Rain*.

Other Famous City Streets

Two other streets stand out at the Studios. As you enter the gates, you walk down **Hollywood Boulevard**. It has lots of shops and is decorated like Hollywood in the 1930s. At the end of the street is a building that looks just like Mann's Chinese Theatre in Hollywood, but it's really The Great Movie Ride.

Nearby is **Sunset Boulevard**. It has an outdoor market and lots of shops. Most are geared more to your parents, but look for Tower of Terror at the end of the street.

> ❝ **I love all the costumes and, of course, the music.** ❞
>
> Nita
> (*age* 14)

Beauty and the Beast Stage Show

Belle, Gaston, Mrs. Potts, Chip, Lumière, Cogsworth, and the Beast come to life in this musical show based on the hit movie. The show opens with "Be Our Guest." Then it backtracks to the beginning of the story, where Belle is unhappy in her small French town. Next, Belle is held captive in the Beast's castle, and later he is attacked by all the townspeople. In the finale, Belle and the Beast declare their love and the wicked spell is broken.

"I especially love when the white doves fly out at the end," says Nita. "I also love the costumes and, of course, the music." Karyn also

loves this show. "There are so many details, like the dancing dishes and spoons," she says.

Some of the kids are not as enthusiastic. "I don't like that the show starts with 'Be Our Guest' so the songs aren't in the same order as in the movie," says Ashley P. "I do like the costumes, though."

Robert agrees. "The songs should be in the same order as in the movie. It's confusing," he says.

Lissy points out that "the singing is really good." Taran says, "If you love the movie, you'll like this show, but I'm not crazy about the movie."

All the kids think that the fighting scene isn't very good. "The fighting parts don't look right—not like fighting at all," says David. Nita agrees. "I don't think little kids would get it that the dancers are supposed to be fighting," she says. "And that scene is so long."

109

You walk for most of the tour, so be sure you have a lot of energy before starting.

Backstage Pass to 101 Dalmatians

Get a behind-the-scenes look at moviemaking during this tour. See how some scenes from the new, live-action version of *101 Dalmatians* were filmed. The tour lasts about 35 minutes, and you walk for most of it. Be sure you have a lot of energy before starting.

The tour begins with a funny film about how dogs were chosen for the roles in the movie. Next you go to the Special Effects Creature Shop to see all kinds of props from the film. Look for the Audio-Animatronics puppies. Without them, many of the action scenes couldn't have been made.

At the Special Effects Stage, you learn that film shot against a blue background can be combined with almost anything from a movie. Two kids from the crowd are chosen to help demonstrate. It's fun to see how their pictures become part of the film.

Then you move on to the soundstages, where you may get to see a real movie being filmed. If not, you'll watch a video about how hard it can be to shoot scenes with hundreds of puppies. The last part of the tour focuses on the villain, Cruella de Vil, and the props that help make her seem so evil. Wait till you see her car!

The Making of...

If you've ever wondered what goes into "the making of" a Disney movie, this attraction is for you. It lets you see the people who provide the voices of the animated stars, and the musicians whose music sets just the right mood. You also learn how many of the sound effects are made.

The attraction changes to keep up with the latest Disney films. While it may take a look at a live-action movie, most often it focuses on an animated feature. Depending on when you go, you may see *The Making of Hercules*, *The Making of The Legend of Mulan*, or another Disney film. We saw *The Making of Toy Story*.

Emma says, "When you watch a movie, you always wonder 'how did they make that sound effect?' and 'how did they draw that?' It's really neat learning how they actually made *Toy Story*. I especially like the sound effects part."

But Adam F. would like to see even more. "I wish they could create a new sound and show you how it's done," he says. Brian F.

Picture yourself here

Picture yourself here

111

likes learning about computer animation. "I didn't know how they made new characters," he says.

Ashley J. thinks "probably grownups would like it more. If you are on a tight schedule, then maybe you shouldn't go to this one. But I learned a lot of things I didn't know about making movies."

Voyage of the Little Mermaid

This live show has all your favorite characters from *The Little Mermaid* acting out the story on stage. Ariel and Prince Eric are played by actors. Flounder, Sebastian, and other sea creatures are played by puppets. The puppeteers are dressed all in black, so it looks like the puppets are suspended in mid-air. A huge Ursula battles with Ariel.

There are some great special effects that really draw you into the show. A screen of water makes you feel like you're under the sea. There are lasers, lightning, and a mist that sprays into the audience. Clips from the movie are also shown on a screen on stage. Several songs are performed to tell the story.

> ## "This is a totally creative show."
> ### Lindsay (age 9)

Dawna thinks "the combination of live actors, puppets, movie clips, lasers, bubbles, and water all add up to a great show."

Adam W. says, "I really like the lasers, and how they make it look like you're underwater." Lindsay agrees. "This is a totally creative show. You feel like you're under the water, especially when you get wet with the mist."

Justin was surprised by the show. "I don't really like *The Little Mermaid*, so I thought it would be stupid. But it ends up being really good," he says.

Tate thinks they leave out too much. "I would like to see a few more scenes added to fill out the story," he says. "Even though most people know what happens, it would be better to have more scenes."

> **It's really neat how they can record sound effects and put them into the movie.**
>
> Adam W. (age 14)

Monster Sound Show

Don't be fooled by the name of the Monster Sound Show. There are no monsters in this show. Instead, audience members are chosen to help create sound effects for a short movie. One person is in charge of the door knocker, someone else takes care of the crashing chandelier, another creates the sound of thunder. Other sound effects include footsteps, a creaking door, wind, and a groaning man.

The short movie, starring Chevy Chase and Martin Short, is shown once with professional sound effects. Then audience members try to fill in and copy the effects when the movie is shown again. The film is shown once more with the new effects. They usually don't match very well, but that's part of the fun.

"It's great to see how some of the sounds in movies are made. There are a lot of mess-ups, and that's really funny," says Lindsay. Adam W. agrees. "It's really neat how they can record sound effects and put them into the movie," he says.

Anna thinks it's fun for both the volunteers and the audience. "The people up on the stage must have the time of their lives, and the audience has a pretty good time, too."

Brad likes the last playback of the movie. "It's cool. When the sounds are supposed to happen there's nothing, and then later you hear the wrong sound," he says.

After the movie, go to the area called SoundWorks, where you can have some hands-on sound effects experiences. "The 3-D room is really fun," says Tate. "Everything sounds like it's actually happening to you." Danielle agrees. "You feel like the people are in the room with you," she says. "You can even hear the guy getting his hair cut."

Disney's The Hunchback of Notre Dame— A Musical Adventure

This newest live show takes you back to 15th-century France, underneath the streets of Paris. You're at a gypsy campsite, about to hear the story of Quasimodo—the hunchback of Notre Dame and star of Disney's latest animated film.

Everything about this show is designed to make you feel part of the action. Ramps stretch out from the stage into the audience, so the actors are right there with you. Together, you travel to the bell tower where Quasimodo is held captive by his evil stepfather. You also visit the streets of Paris just in time for the Festival of Fools.

If you've seen the movie, you'll recognize all the characters in the show. The narrator is Clopin, King of the Gypsies. He receives lots of help from his colorful band of gypsy players, who sing, dance, and act

117

out the tale. You also meet Quasimodo; his stepfather, Judge Claude Frollo; Esmeralda, the beautiful gypsy girl whom Quasimodo loves; and Phoebus, the kind soldier who becomes Quasimodo's friend. And, of course, there are the wacky gargoyles, Victor, Hugo, and Laverne.

If you didn't see the movie, you'll still enjoy this show. The gypsies tell you everything you need to know. They're wonderful guides who know the story, and the streets of Paris, inside and out. They also have plenty of tricks—and special effects--to keep you on your toes.

Look for the live birds that fly into the sky when Quasimodo

appears in his bell tower. Keep your eye on Esmeralda, who disappears in a puff of smoke and reappears on the other side of the stage.

A highlight of the show is the Festival of Fools. This celebration is packed with dancers and puppets, all in bright costumes. They're singing and laughing, and seem to be having the time of their lives. This scene sets the tone for the whole show, which is a lot like a street fair. That makes it different from any other live performance at the Disney-MGM Studios. It also makes it a lot of fun.

Attraction Ratings

AWESOME (See at Least Twice)

REALLY COOL (Don't Miss)

COOL (Check It Out)

YAWN (Save for Last)

- Jim Henson's Muppet*Vision 3-D
- Star Tours
- Indiana Jones Epic Stunt Spectacular
- Tower of Terror

- The Magic of Disney Animation
- SuperStar Television
- Monster Sound Show
- Voyage of the Little Mermaid
- The Hunchback of Notre Dame show (Sounds like a winner!)
- Backstage Pass to 101 Dalmatians

- Beauty and the Beast Stage Show
- The Great Movie Ride
- Studio Backlot Tour
- The Making of...
- Honey, I Shrunk the Kids Movie Set Adventure

- No yawns here!

My visit to Disney-MGM Studios will include...

Everything Else in the World

When most kids think about Walt Disney World, they think of the Magic Kingdom, Epcot, and Disney-MGM Studios. But as we discovered on our trips, there's much more to see.

There's a petting farm with baby animals, a wooded campground with a water park known as River Country, a pair of new miniature golf courses, two state-of-the-art water parks called Typhoon Lagoon and Blizzard Beach, lakes where you can rent boats, the Disney Village Marketplace, a behind-the-scenes program called Wonders of Walt Disney World, and lots of restaurants and hotels.

In this chapter, you can read about all these extras and decide which ones you most want to see. The kids agree that renting Water Sprites for a ride on one of Walt Disney World's waterways is a great break from the theme park routine. And spending time at one of the water parks is always a fun way to cool off.

So read on and help your family decide where to stay, where to eat, and which added attractions to visit.

Fort Wilderness

Tucked away in a wooded area of Walt Disney World is Fort Wilderness. You can stay overnight in trailers or just come for a day. There are tennis and volleyball courts, and a marina with lots of boats. River Country, described on page 126, is also here.

You could spend days here and not see everything. If you only have a couple of hours, explore the petting farm and rent Water Sprites for a ride around Bay Lake.

Petting Farm

This small farm is home to some extra-friendly animals, including goats, sheep, chickens, and pigs, and ponies that you can ride.

Most of the kids think that the farm can be fun at any age. "It gives you a chance to get close to the animals without being afraid," says Lissy. Robert especially likes "letting the baby goats chew on my fingers."

Karyn says petting farms can be boring for older kids, but "if you really like animals, you'll have fun no matter how old you are."

More Fun

There are many other activities at Fort Wilderness. You can rent a canoe ($4 per hour) for a trip along the campground's canals. Or you can rent a bicycle ($3 per hour) and explore one of the many trails. At the Tri-Circle-D Ranch, you can see the champion horses that pull the trolleys in the Magic Kingdom. Kids 9 and over can take a horseback trail ride ($17 for the 45-minute trip). There are hayrides that last about an hour and cost $4

for kids (ages 3 to 9) and $6 for adults. You can also go on a fishing trip, or just fish in the canals.

Water Sprites

These small motor boats don't go very fast, but they sure feel like they do. The wind whips in your face and the nose of the boat lifts into the air, giving you a great sense of speed.

A Water Sprite trip on Bay Lake gets very high marks from all the kids. The rental is for 30 minutes, so you can cover a lot of water. "It's awesome," says Brian L. "I was turning into the waves and one splashed on top of me." David thinks it's neat to drive your own boat. "This is fun that you definitely can't miss," he says.

For Lissy, the Water Sprites are "loads of fun, and being in the

water really cools you off." Karyn likes the scenery around the lake. "It's really pretty with all the trees," she says.

Some kids want the boats to go faster, but Nita says, "It's not too fast and not too slow."

Where to Rent Water Sprites

You can also rent Water Sprites at resorts like the Contemporary, Polynesian, Grand Floridian, Wilderness Lodge, and Caribbean Beach, plus at the Disney Village Marketplace. The cost is $15 for a half hour. You must be 12 years old to drive, except at the Marketplace, where you must be 14 years old.

Fantasia Gardens

If you've seen the movie *Fantasia*, you'll know right away how this new miniature golf course got its name. The same characters who danced their way through the famous Walt Disney film make this different from any other miniature golf experience. Where else will you find hippos on tiptoe, dancing mushrooms, or xylophone stairs?

Fantasia Gardens Miniature Golf is located near the Dolphin, Swan, and BoardWalk resorts. It's really two courses: Fantasia Gardens and Fantasia Fairways. The first is an 18-hole miniature golf course that the entire family will enjoy. The second is more difficult. It's designed for older kids and adults.

Each hole at Fantasia Gardens is designed to look like a scene from *Fantasia*. Music from the movie is also piped in. Best of all are the surprises in store for you as your ball makes its way along the course.

The holes are grouped by musical themes. Play through the cave at a Pastoral Symphony hole, and a bat appears on the wall. At a Dance of the Hours hole, pay close attention to the hippo standing on the alligator's back. Hit your ball through the alligator's mouth, and the hippo dances. At The Sorcerer's Apprentice hole, the brooms are just as busy as in the movie. But this time, they dump their water on the golf course.

Both courses are open from 10 A.M. to midnight, although that may vary. The cost is about $8 for adults and $7 for kids ages 3 to 9.

Waters of the World

Walt Disney World is a water wonderland. With three spectacular water parks and the unique swimming pools at the resorts, getting wet, staying cool, and having fun at Walt Disney World is very easy. If you want to go swimming, try to avoid January and February. Even Florida weather can be cool during these months. Here's a description of the water parks and some of the special pools so you can decide which you'd like to try out most.

Typhoon Lagoon

This watery playground is a great place to spend a whole day. The surf lagoon is larger than two football fields, and the 4½-foot waves make body surfing fun. There are two speed slides that send you through a cave at 30 miles per hour, a couple of winding slides, and a white-water slide that gives groups and families a chance to ride the rapids together. There's also a special area just for younger children called

Arrive at the water parks as soon as they open or wait until late afternoon.

124

Ketchakiddee Creek, which has smaller slides and other games.

On top of Mt. Mayday, the mountain in the center of Typhoon Lagoon, there's a boat called the *Miss Tilly*. Keep an eye on the smokestack on top of the boat. It shoots a flume of water every 30 minutes. If you climb to the top of Mt. Mayday, you get a great view of all the pools and slides at Typhoon Lagoon.

The biggest water slides are two speed slides called Humunga Cowabunga. Castaway Creek is a stream that circles the entire park. You can hop in an oversize tube and float along with the current. There are lots of props along the way, and you can get in and out of the creek at many locations.

There's also a volleyball court, a shop, two restaurants, and lots of lounge chairs for your parents.

Blizzard Beach

T his water park offers the most thrills, with some of the World's longest, fastest slides. It also has plenty of activities for those who like less excitement. "This is one awesome water park," says Karyn. "Everything is so detailed and exciting."

Blizzard Beach was designed to look like a ski resort. And like a ski resort, everything centers around the mountain—in this case, the 90-foot-high Mt. Gushmore. On top of the mountain is a tower that gives you a view of all the action below. Or, get a floating tour on Cross Country Creek, a raft ride that slowly circles the entire park.

The biggest thrill at Blizzard Beach is Summit Plummet. This ride begins 120 feet in the air, on a platform that looks like a ski jump. It sends you down a 350-foot slide at about 60 miles per hour. That's as fast as most cars on the highway.

Slush Gusher is a speed slide that also takes you down Mt. Gushmore,

Hot Tip

Bring water shoes. The ground gets awfully hot and so do your feet!

but not quite as fast. Other activities—including tube slides, body slides, and inner-tube rides—keep you busy all day. When you're ready to relax, try the free-form pool. Its gentle waves make it great for swimming or just hanging out.

For preteens, there's Ski Patrol Training Center, featuring a slide, an "iceberg" obstacle course, and ropes for swinging over and into the water. For younger kids, there's Tike's Peak, with a smaller version of Mt. Gushmore's slides and a snow-castle fountain play area.

River Country

If you've ever read *The Adventures of Tom Sawyer* or *The Adventures of Huckleberry Finn*, River Country will seem like it came right from those stories. Disney Imagineers have created a swimming hole just like the ones Tom and Huck used to visit—only this one is much bigger. It has a huge swimming pool with two steep water slides. The main section of River Country is Bay Cove, an area with rope swings, a ship's boom, and other things made for swinging on and jumping into the water. Bay Cove also has two flume rides that send you down a corkscrew path into the water.

Other River Country activities include a white-water ride in a large inner tube, an area with smaller slides and water toys for younger kids, and a small beach. There's also a small snack stand.

Let's Get Wet!

There are many other places around Walt Disney World that offer chances to get wet. At the Magic Kingdom, head for Splash Mountain and sit in the front row. Or hang around Donald's (leaky) Boat at Mickey's Toontown Fair. At Epcot, you can spend hours playing at the jumping fountains outside Journey Into Imagination and on the pathway between Future World and World Showcase. At the Disney-MGM Studios, the Studio Backlot Tour provides a splash during Catastrophe Canyon (sit on the left for a wetter ride), and the leaky hoses at the Honey, I Shrunk the Kids Movie Set Adventure playground spurt water unexpectedly. At the Disney Village Marketplace, there are several places where water jets shoot up from the ground.

Check out the water-spouting elephants at BoardWalk.

Hotel Pools

There are some great pools at the Walt Disney World resorts. You're allowed to swim in the pools only if you're a guest of the hotel. So read this section carefully, and read the rest of the hotel information later in this chapter starting on page 139. Then you can give your family advice on where you'd like to stay.

One of the best pools is Stormalong Bay at the Yacht Club and Beach Club resorts. There's a sunken ship with a built-in water slide so you can climb the wreck and slide back down to the water. At Port Orleans, Doubloon Lagoon is a pool built around a sea serpent. His tail juts out in spots along the walkways, and the water slide is his tongue. Ol' Man Island is a 3½-acre recreation center at Dixie Landings. Its large pool has slides and ropes.

At the Polynesian resort, the Swimming Pool Lagoon is surrounded by a large cluster of boulders that is actually a water slide. The Grotto Pool between the Dolphin and Swan hotels is a group of connecting pools with bridges and a water slide. At the All-Star Sports resort, the main pool looks like an ocean with circling sharks. At the All-Star Music resort, one pool is in the shape of a guitar and the other is in the shape of a piano.

The new pool at the Contemporary resort has water jets and a water slide. At the new BoardWalk resort, try the Luna Park pool. It's designed to look like an amusement park, and features water-spouting elephants and the Keister Coaster water slide.

Restaurant Guide

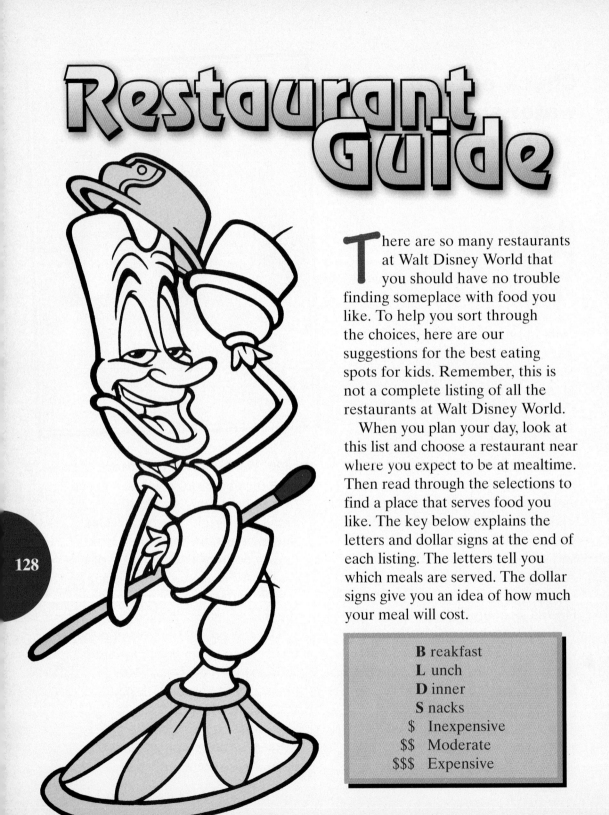

There are so many restaurants at Walt Disney World that you should have no trouble finding someplace with food you like. To help you sort through the choices, here are our suggestions for the best eating spots for kids. Remember, this is not a complete listing of all the restaurants at Walt Disney World.

When you plan your day, look at this list and choose a restaurant near where you expect to be at mealtime. Then read through the selections to find a place that serves food you like. The key below explains the letters and dollar signs at the end of each listing. The letters tell you which meals are served. The dollar signs give you an idea of how much your meal will cost.

B reakfast
L unch
D inner
S nacks
$ Inexpensive
$$ Moderate
$$$ Expensive

Magic Kingdom

Sit-down Restaurants

Crystal Palace: Main Street. Daily character buffets. Pasta, fish, chicken, salads. $$$. B, L, D.

King Stefan's Banquet Hall: Fantasyland. Daily character breakfast. At lunch and dinner, prime rib, roast beef, chicken, salads. $$$. B, L, D.

Liberty Tree Tavern: Liberty Square. Daily all-you-can-eat character dinner. Seafood, chicken, prime rib, sandwiches, salads. $$$. L, D.

Tony's Town Square: Main Street. Pizza, spaghetti with meatballs, Italian sandwiches. $$$. B, L, D.

Fast Food

Aunt Polly's Landing: Tom Sawyer Island. Sandwiches, soft-serve ice cream, lemonade. $. L, S.

Columbia Harbour House: Liberty Square. Seafood, sandwiches, salads. $. L, D, S.

Cosmic Ray's Starlight Café: Tomorrowland. Soups, salads, burgers, sandwiches, chicken. $. L, D, S.

Diamond Horseshoe Saloon Revue: Frontierland. Western show. Sandwiches, chips. $. L, S.

Lumière's Kitchen: Fantasyland. Chicken nuggets, grilled cheese, cookies. $. L, D, S.

Pecos Bill Café: Frontierland. Burgers, barbecued chicken sandwiches, hot dogs. $. L, D, S.

Pinocchio Village Haus: Fantasyland. Burgers, hot dogs, sandwiches, salads. $. L, D, S.

Snack Spots

Auntie Gravity's Galactic Goodies: Tomorrowland. Frozen yogurt, fresh fruit. $. S.

Liberty Square Market: Liberty Square. Fresh fruit. $. S.

Mrs. Potts' Cupboard: Fantasyland. Sundaes, floats. $. S.

Plaza Ice Cream Parlor: Main Street. Lots of flavors. $. S.

Sunshine Tree Terrace: Adventureland. Orange slush, frozen yogurt shakes. $. S.

Westward Ho: Frontierland. Cookies, pretzels, chips. $. S.

Epcot

Future World

Sit-down Restaurants
Coral Reef: The Living Seas. Seafood, pasta, chicken. $$$. L, D.
Garden Grill: The Land. Daily character meals. Chicken tenders, macaroni and cheese, french fries. $$ to $$$. B, L, D.

Fast Food
Electric Umbrella: Innoventions. Burgers, chicken sandwiches, hot dogs, salads, frozen yogurt. $. L, D, S.
Pasta Piazza Ristorante: Innoventions. Pizza, pasta. $. B, L, D, S.
Pure & Simple: Wonders of Life. Waffles with fruit toppings, sandwiches, salads. $. B, L, S.
Sunshine Season Food Fair: The Land. Food court. $. B, L, D, S.

World Showcase

Sit-down Restaurants
Au Petit Café: France. Salads, pasta, filled croissants, sandwiches. $$. L, D, S.
Biergarten: Germany. Chicken, frankfurters, sausages, potato pancakes. $$ to $$$. L, D.
L'Originale Alfredo di Roma Ristorante: Italy. Pasta, chicken, veal. $$$. L, D.
Marrakesh: Morocco. Chicken bastila (cinnamon chicken in pastry), sampler platters. $$$. L, D.
San Angel Inn: Mexico. Tortillas, chicken, guacamole, tacos. $$$. L, D.
Teppanyaki Dining Rooms: Japan. Stir-fried meat, vegetables, and fish cooked at the table. $$$. L, D.

Fast Food
Cantina de San Angel: Mexico. Burritos, tortillas with chicken, tacos, nachos. $. L, D, S.
Kringla Bakeri og Kafé: Norway. Sandwiches, pastries. $. L, S.
Liberty Inn: The American Adventure. Burgers, hot dogs, chicken sandwiches, fries, ice cream. $. L, D, S.
Lotus Blossom Café: China. Sweet-and-sour pork, stir-fried beef, egg rolls, soup. $. L, D.

Sommerfest: Germany. Bratwurst sandwiches, soft pretzels, apple strudel. $. L, D, S.
Yakitori House: Japan. Yakitori (skewered chicken), teriyaki sandwiches. $. L, D, S.

Snack Spots
Boulangerie Pâtisserie: France. Pastries, croissants, éclairs, chocolate mousse. $. S.
Refreshment Outpost: Between Germany and China. Frozen yogurt or ice cream. $. S.
Refreshment Port: Canada. Frozen yogurt, cookies, fresh fruit. $. S.

Disney-MGM Studios

Sit-down Restaurants
50's Prime Time Café: Macaroni and cheese, burgers, tuna salad sandwiches, chicken pot pie, hot roast beef, alphabet soup, ice cream sodas, shakes. $$. L, D, S.
Mama Melrose's Ristorante Italiano: Pizza, lasagne, meatball subs, chicken, pasta. $$ to $$$. L, D (dinner offered seasonally).
Sci-Fi Dine-In Theater: Burgers, huge hot and cold sandwiches, pasta, salads. $$ to $$$. L, D.

> ## "No matter how old you are, you can become a kid at the 50's Prime Time Café. "
>
> Nita
> (age 14)

Soundstage: Daily character buffets. Macaroni and cheese, hot dogs, chicken tenders. $$ to $$$. B, L, D.

Fast Food
Backlot Express: Chicken, burgers, hot dogs, salads. $. L, D, S.
Commissary: Sandwiches, burgers, salads. $. L, D.
Hollywood & Vine: Roasted chicken, spaghetti and meatballs, ribs, salads. $ to $$. B, L, D.

Snack Spots
Dinosaur Gertie's: Frozen slush drinks, fruit yogurt bars, frozen bananas. $. S.
Studio Catering Co.: Fresh fruit, sundaes, milk shakes. $. S.

Food Courts

Food courts make it easy to satisfy everyone in your family at mealtimes. Among the ones we tried is Old Port Royale at the Caribbean Beach resort. Its six counters serve everything from pizza and pasta to burgers, sandwiches, and chicken. For dessert, there's a bakery that also serves ice cream. The kids like being able to choose their own meals. Brian L. says, "There are a lot of good things to eat. I love all the selections." Ashley P. agrees. "I especially like the pizza," she says.

Other hotel food courts are at Port Orleans, Dixie Landings, All-Star Sports, and All-Star Music resorts. In Epcot, you'll find the Sunshine Season Food Fair in The Land pavilion.

Eating With the Characters

Kids of all ages enjoy eating with the characters— especially since it's so easy to have your picture taken with them. As David says, "Seeing all the Disney characters joke and dance around makes breakfast special." In fact, dining with the characters is so popular that lots of restaurants offer chances for you to share a meal with your favorites. No matter which restaurant you choose, it's a good idea to make priority seating arrangements ahead of time. Just call 407-WDW-DINE.

At the Resorts

Captain Mickey and his crew host one of the biggest character breakfasts at Fulton's Crab House, near Pleasure Island and the Disney Village Marketplace. You can also eat breakfast with Mary Poppins at 1900 Park Fare in the Grand Floridian, with Admiral Goofy at Cape May Café in the Beach Club, with Winnie the Pooh and friends at Olivia's Café in Old Key West, and with characters from *Pocahontas* at Artist Point in the Wilderness Lodge.

Characters can also be found at breakfast at 'Ohana in the Polynesian and at Garden Grove

Most restaurants, including fast-food stands, also serve healthy foods such as salads, fresh fruit, broiled or grilled chicken breast, turkey burgers, and nonfat frozen yogurt.

in the Swan (Saturday only). For Sunday brunch, try Harry's Safari Bar & Grille in the Dolphin.

Chef Mickey serves up breakfast and dinner at Chef Mickey's restaurant in the Contemporary. Other dinner choices include 1900 Park Fare in the Grand Floridian and Gulliver's Grill at Garden Grove in the Swan (Monday, Thursday, Friday).

In the Theme Parks

The theme parks get in on the fun, too, with character meals throughout the day. In the Magic Kingdom, Cinderella hosts the "Once Upon a Time" breakfast at King Stefan's Banquet Hall. Winnie the Pooh entertains at the Crystal Palace buffet all day long. Or have dinner with Goofy at the Liberty Tree Tavern.

Eat at Soundstage to meet the latest characters.

In Epcot, visit Chip 'n' Dale for any meal at the Garden Grill. In the Disney-MGM Studios, the Soundstage restaurant is the place to be for a meal with characters from recent animated films. Look for your friends from *The Hunchback of Notre Dame*, *Pocahontas*, *Aladdin*, and *Beauty and the Beast*.

Hot Tip

Ask about portion sizes or you may get way too much food.

Kids' Favorites

Although almost every restaurant at Walt Disney World caters to kids, our group definitely has its favorites. At the top of the list is Planet Hollywood near Pleasure Island. "If you like movies, this is the place to be," says Dawna. "The bus from *Speed* is hanging from the ceiling! Movie scenes run on a big screen. And everything tastes great."

Whispering Canyon Café in the Wilderness Lodge is also a big hit. "Dinner is incredible," says Karyn. Lindsay likes "how they bring all the food out and you help yourself."

The kids recommend Chef Mickey's in the Contemporary resort, where you get a big selection at the buffet and a chance to meet Mickey Mouse. Brian F. says, "I like it when the characters come up to your table." Save room for the ice cream sundae bar. "You can make whatever you want, and get as much as you want," he adds.

For a quick bite in the Magic Kingdom, try Pecos Bill Café. Karyn says, "The Wild West setting is fun, and the food is great." Taran agrees. "My chicken sandwich was awesome, and we got the food fast," he says.

If you have more time, Tony's Town Square on Main Street is a good choice for kids and parents. Dawna says, "This is where Lady and Tramp ate. I had spaghetti and meatballs just like they did."

For fast food in Epcot, try Pasta Piazza in Future World. "The pizza is excellent, even though the pieces are a little big," says Tate. The kids also like the Liberty Inn in World Showcase. "The food is good," says Brad. "There's a little more selection than usual. I had chili."

Snack Wagons

All around the theme parks are wagons that sell soft drinks, popcorn, and lots of ice cream —Cookies 'n' Cream ice cream sandwiches, Mouseketeer Bars, low-fat yogurt, and strawberry bars. Some wagons offer fresh fruit and other healthy snacks.

Emma prefers the all-you-can-eat meal at the Garden Grill. "It's a wonderful place to eat, and Minnie, Mickey, and Chip 'n' Dale are there," she says. Adam F. enjoys the tasty chicken and fries. Ashley J. likes the dessert. "They have 'dirt' cups with gummy worms!" she says.

At the Disney-MGM Studios, the Sci-Fi Dine-In Theater gets rave reviews. Dawna says, "It's set up like a drive-in movie theater. You sit in a car with a table and there are old science-fiction movies showing." Anna adds, "The waitresses are even on skates."

The kids agree that the 50's Prime Time Café at the Disney-MGM Studios is one of their top choices. David says, "I've never had so much fun in a restaurant in my entire life."

Eating at the Hotels

Most of the Walt Disney World resorts have several restaurants. Here's our list of the best spots for kids in each hotel.

All-Star Sports and All-Star Music
• End Zone and Intermission food courts

BoardWalk
• Spoodles

Caribbean Beach
• Old Port Royale food court

Contemporary
• Chef Mickey's

Dixie Landings
• Colonel's Cotton Mill food court

Dolphin
• Coral Café

Fort Wilderness Campground
• Trail's End Buffet

Grand Floridian
• 1900 Park Fare

Old Key West
• Olivia's Café

Polynesian
• 'Ohana

Port Orleans
• Sassagoula Floatworks & Food Factory

Swan
• Garden Grove Café

Wilderness Lodge
• Whispering Canyon Café

Yacht Club and Beach Club
• Beaches & Cream Soda Shop

Lissy thinks "it's so neat how the waitresses and waiters pretend to be Mom and Dad." Nita picks this as the best choice for both parents and kids. "No matter how old you are, you can become a kid at the 50's Prime Time Café," she says.

Of course, all restaurants can't please everybody. Keep in mind the type of food you like when making your choice. That's where our Restaurant Guide can help.

All the kids agree that the buffet-style clambake at Cape May Café in the Beach Club resort is a good choice for lots of different tastes. Danielle likes that "they have something for everyone. There are different kinds of seafood, but also salads, pasta, and chicken." Lindsay says, "If you can't find something here, you won't find it anywhere."

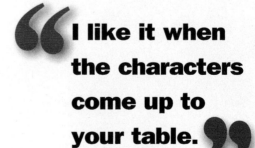

I like it when the characters come up to your table.

Brian F. (age 10)

"They get everyone in on the fun."

Danielle (age 11)

Dinner Shows

At the Hoop-Dee-Doo Musical Revue, a group of entertainers sings, dances, and tells jokes while you eat a dinner of fried chicken, ribs, and corn-on-the-cob. Danielle says, "They get everyone in on the fun and put on a wonderful show." David thinks the show is "very funny. I was laughing the whole time." Tate says, "Anybody in the Orlando area should go see it. It's the perfect combination of great food and entertainment."

Other dinner shows include the Polynesian Luau and Mickey's

GUEST CHECK

Restaurants I'd like to try:

Tropical Revue at the Polynesian resort. The Biergarten at Epcot's Germany pavilion features a show with traditional German musicians. Reservations for these shows must be made well in advance by calling 407-WDW-DINE.

Walt Disney World Resorts

There are 17 resorts around the Walt Disney World property. That means there are enough rooms at Walt Disney World for you to stay in a different spot every night for almost 58 years!

We visited most of the resorts during our trips. Here are brief descriptions of all the resorts at Walt Disney World. There's information on the things that are most important to kids, like arcades, restaurants, special programs, and activities. For more details about the hotel pools, see page 127.

Near the Magic Kingdom

Contemporary: The monorail rides through the center of this modern-style hotel. There are three restaurants, two pools, boat rentals, seven shops, and a huge arcade. "If you love to play video games, you'll love this place," says Ashley P. The kids also like that the monorail travels right through the building.

Polynesian: The decor here looks like it comes straight from the South Seas, with beautiful plants and trees all around. There are three restaurants, two pools, boat rentals, an arcade, and six shops. "The Polynesian has a beautiful beach," says Brian L. And Nita and David like the pool with its big slide.

Grand Floridian: At first, this elegant hotel seems to be designed for grownups only, but it's fun for kids, too. There's a pool, boat rentals, a playground, an arcade, four shops, and six restaurants.

Wilderness Lodge: With its log columns and totem poles, this hotel offers a taste of the American West. "You really feel like you're in the wilderness," says Lindsay. Dawna likes that "people sit in rocking chairs just watching the fire—in Florida!" This hotel has two restaurants, a pool, bike and boat rentals, an arcade, and a special Cubs Den program for kids.

Fort Wilderness Resort & Campground: Guests can either camp with their own equipment or rent a trailer home at this wooded campground. There are two pools, two restaurants, a large beach, boat and bicycle rentals, a petting farm, pony rides, and two arcades.

Near Epcot and the Studios

Caribbean Beach: The rooms at this hotel are located in many colorful buildings. There's one main pool, plus many smaller pools, a food court, boat and bicycle rentals, a small arcade, and one shop. "It's a pretty hotel because of all the colors," says Nita.

Yacht Club and Beach Club: These are two connected hotels. One has a boating theme and the other has a beach theme. There's a large main pool, plus two smaller ones, boat rentals, five restaurants, an ice cream parlor, an arcade, and two shops.

" **The All-Star resort is the coolest place.** "

Ashley J. (age 12)

Dolphin and Swan: You can't miss the giant dolphin and swan statues on top of these two hotels. They're similar because they were designed by the same architect. The Dolphin has six restaurants, an ice cream parlor, an arcade, four shops, and Camp Dolphin, a program just for kids. "Camp Dolphin is great and the rooms are very nice," says Ashley P. The Swan has three restaurants, a small arcade, Camp Swan, and one shop. The hotels share three pools and boat rentals.

BoardWalk: This hotel is right on the boardwalk, along with a bakery, sweet shop, and lots of restaurants and shops. It has an arcade and a great pool modeled after an amusement park. There's also a fun mini golf course nearby.

Port Orleans: The special details at this hotel make it look like the city it's named for, New Orleans. There's one restaurant and a food

court, a large specially designed pool, boat and bicycle rentals, an arcade, and a shop.

Dixie Landings: Next door to Port Orleans, this hotel represents the countryside surrounding New Orleans. There's one restaurant and a food court, a large pool on a recreation island, plus five more pools, boat and bicycle rentals, an arcade, and a shop.

Old Key West: The townhouses that make up this resort are more like homes. There are two restaurants, one main pool, plus smaller pools around the resort, a small arcade, boat and bicycle rentals, and a shop. There are VCRs in the rooms and movie rentals available. Karyn thinks it "would be a nice place to stay for a while because it's so homey."

The Villas at the Disney Institute: There are several types of villas, including "treehouses" on stilts. There's one restaurant, six pools, bicycle rentals, and a small arcade.

All-Star Resorts: Sports and music fans should head for these two resorts. All-Star Sports has five buildings, each designed around a different sport—tennis, football, surfing, baseball, or basketball. At All-Star Music the buildings are themed around five types of music—rock and roll, calypso, Broadway tunes, country-and-western, and jazz. Each hotel has a food court, playground, large arcade, and two pools. Ashley J. says, "The All-Star resort is the coolest place. It's so colorful." Lindsay adds, "The arcades have every game you could imagine."

Entertainment

There's always entertainment going on at Walt Disney World. When you arrive in each theme park, pick up a guidemap so you can decide what to see. Here are descriptions of some of the best shows.

THE MAGIC KINGDOM

SpectroMagic: Every night of this anniversary year, this parade makes its way down Main Street. Advanced technology such as holograms, special lighting, and a state-of-the-art sound system creates a show that, as Dawna says, "no one should miss. It's a perfect way to end an evening

or a trip." Lindsay agrees. "The dazzling lights make it gorgeous."

25th Anniversary Parade: This parade celebrating Walt Disney World's 25th year features all of your favorite Disney characters. Mickey and pals want all the park guests to share in the excitement of this party, so visitors can take part in the parade. Each float will also burst out with a surprise, like confetti or fireworks. See our special section starting on page 9 to learn more.

Fantasy in the Sky Fireworks: Even those who don't like fireworks can't keep their eyes off this display. The show is presented nightly. It uses about 200 shells—all set off within five minutes to create fantastic bursts of color. Ashley J. says, "It lights up the sky!"

Kids of the Kingdom: This group performs often in the Castle Forecourt. The show has lively singing and dancing to Disney tunes—plus appearances by Disney characters. Danielle says, "The dancers are great and so are the characters." Justin offers this advice: "If you don't get a chance to see a lot of the characters, then go to this show."

142

EPCOT

IllumiNations 25: A spectacular laser, water, and fireworks show with a 25th anniversary twist takes place each night around World Showcase Lagoon. In the new finale, fireworks create the image of a birthday cake in the sky. "The lights, lasers, and fireworks are really cool," says Lissy. Adam W. likes "how the fountains go up and down." You can see the show from anywhere around the lagoon.

Kids Weekends: For a few special weekends each year, every World Showcase nation offers special hands-on activities. Each weekend is different, but the theme is always the same: All kids, no matter where they live, like to have fun. Past events have included paper lantern and fan making in China, face painting in Canada, Alice's Tea Party in the United Kingdom, watercoloring in France, LEGO tables in Norway, macaroni art in Italy, piñata decorating in Mexico, sporting contests in The American Adventure, and origami (paper folding) in Japan. Check a guidemap to see if an event is planned during your visit.

DISNEY-MGM STUDIOS

Sorcery in the Sky Fireworks: During the summer and holiday seasons, you can see the World's most amazing fireworks, set to music from Hollywood's biggest films, including Disney's *Fantasia*. Check your guidemap to see if it's happening during your visit.

Toy Story Parade: Every afternoon, the characters from *Toy Story* come to life in their own parade. Buzz Lightyear rides a float surrounded by martians. Woody shares a float with Rex the Dinosaur and Mike, the Rockin' Robot Radio Tape Recorder. The kids love this parade. Brian F. says, "It has soldiers, Buzz, Woody, Mr. Potato Head, and Rex standing up high on lots of games." The green army men are a big favorite. "I like them and the aliens the best," says Ashley J.

143

Wonders of the World

Kids ages 10 through 15 with a special interest in art, entertainment, international culture, or the environment can sign up for a six-hour backstage learning adventure. There are four programs to choose from. We got a special tour with a brief overview of two of them.

Art Magic: Bringing Illusion to Life shows how artists at Walt Disney World create the illusion of reality in movies and the theme parks. This adventure includes a behind-the-scenes look at the animation process. You get to paint your own animation cel. You also learn about the use of theme, color,

and forced perspective. At the end of the day, you get a chance to draw your own Disney characters, using secret tips shared during your backstage adventure.

"If you really want to know how they make a cartoon or create animation, this is the place to go," says Justin. Dawna agrees. "I like the animation part the best," she says, "because you get to see all of the steps it takes to make a movie, and a hands-on chance to try it yourself."

Show Biz Magic: The Walt Disney World of Entertainment introduces you to the wide range of entertainment at Walt Disney World. You discover the importance of communication, show preparation, auditions, being a good audience, and star qualities. You learn firsthand by talking with performers. Highlights include a visit to the wig and makeup room located in a tunnel beneath the Magic Kingdom.

All the kids found something to like about this adventure. "I think everybody should go to this because it explains what goes on behind the

scenes," says Tate. Lindsay thinks "it's exciting to see how they get the live characters ready with wigs and makeup." Adam W. says, "I love this program. It's really neat how we learned about the parade floats and how they work."

Passport: A Secret Mission to Other Lands brings to life the traditions, art, culture, and history of the countries in Epcot's World Showcase. You travel from land to land, talking with international cast members and learning about different types of architecture. You also find out how to communicate in other languages, decode ancient hieroglyphics, and uncover the secrets of world-famous landmarks.

Wildlife Adventure: Exploring the Environment takes you on a safari through the Walt Disney World conservation area. You take part in discussions on wildlife identification, ecosystems, and environmental issues. You also get to observe creatures in their natural habitat.

The cost is $79 for each program. It includes access to the theme parks and backstage areas during each program, lunch, and a personalized certificate of completion. For reservations, call 407-354-1855.

Shopping

It's easy to get overwhelmed by the number of shops at Walt Disney World. Shopping is an important part of your vacation, but you should decide in advance how much you can spend.

Most kids bring some of their own money. Dawna suggests saving up to buy souvenirs because "some things are really expensive." Whether you're spending your own money or your parents', be careful not to buy the first thing you see. You're bound to find something you like better later on. A good place to shop is the Disney Village Marketplace. "Everything you'd want is right there," says Dawna.

Here are some suggestions for souvenirs in several price ranges. Keep in mind that these prices are subject to change.

Under $5

Buttons	$ 1.50
Magnets	$ 2.75
Mousketeer ears	$ 4.25
Pins	$ 4.95
Keychains	$ 4.95

Under $10

Wallets	$ 5.95
Sunglasses	$ 5.98
Character banks	$ 6.95
Minnie ears	$ 7.95
Waist pouches	$ 9.95

Under $20

WDW calendars	$10.95
Stuffed characters	$10.95
Mickey gloves	$12.95
Hair scrunchies	$12.95
Baseball caps	$14.95
Plush hats	$14.95
Tote bags	$14.95
T-shirts	$16.95
Clocks	$18.00
Backpacks	$18.95

Under $25

Classic videos	$21.99
Sweatshirts	$22.00
Stuffed characters	$22.95
Watches	$24.95

Hot Tips

In this chapter, we'll give you advice on how to get the most out of your Walt Disney World trip. There are lots of planning suggestions, plus hints on making a schedule, getting along with your family, finding the characters, and many other tips the kids discovered on our trips. You may want to take notes as you go along since there's a lot to remember. There's also an explanation of the Disney lingo used in this book. So read on for some hot tips from the kids for the most awesome vacation in the World!

GETTING READY TO GO
When to Go

Deciding when to visit Walt Disney World can be confusing. Karyn warns that "you can't do anything when it's really crowded." Nita says, "If you're not a person who likes crowds, go during the winter. In the summer the lines are long for everything." Brian L. agrees. "Definitely don't go during a holiday when school is out."

To avoid crowds, try to visit during the first two weeks in December. The weather is still nice, and you can see all the Christmas shows and decorations. If the only

time you can visit is during a school vacation or in the summer, allow plenty of extra time. And plan your days carefully so you don't spend your entire vacation in line.

During less crowded times, especially in January, attractions may be closed for renovations. And if you want to go swimming, avoid January and February, when it's often too cool. Also, the water parks usually close for renovations sometime during the winter.

Write for more information:
**Walt Disney World
Box 10,000
Lake Buena Vista,
Florida 32830**

148

Packing Tips

When you pack, make sure you're prepared for either warm or cool weather. Layers are a good idea, so you can take something off if you get hot. You don't need dressy clothes. Shorts or jeans and T-shirts are fine for just about everywhere. Here's a list to get you started:

- This book
- Activities to keep you busy on the plane or in the car—books, magazines, puzzles, or hand-held video games
- A sweatshirt or sweater
- Shorts and jeans
- Long-sleeved and short-sleeved shirts
- Bathing suits
- Broken-in sneakers or shoes
- Sunscreen and a hat
- Camera and extra film
- Backpack for your stuff

My Packing List

My Visit to Walt Disney World

Day 1

Day 2

Day 3

Day 4

Day 5

MAKING A SCHEDULE

The kids agree that you should definitely make a schedule. Karyn says, "It doesn't have to be that detailed, just planned out so you basically know what you want to do. I would use this guide to plan out the whole trip before leaving home." Anna agrees. "There's no way you'll get to see everything. This book will help you decide beforehand your 'must-sees.'"

Ashley P. suggests that you also "sit down with your parents and see what everyone else wants to do." Nita agrees. "Work with your parents on the schedule, so you all get to do the things you want to do." Robert advises that "the book is your best tour guide because it tells you about all the rides. If it says The Haunted Mansion is scary and you don't like scary rides, then you know not to go on it."

First you should decide how many days to spend in each park. The kids agree that the ideal trip would last about ten days. They also agree that the minimum amount of time for a Walt Disney World vacation is about five days. You need at least two days for the Magic Kingdom, two days for Epcot, and a full day for the Disney-MGM Studios. Tate suggests, "Go to the Magic Kingdom first, then to the Disney-MGM Studios, and then to Epcot."

Karyn suggests "including a day of swimming and relaxing. Don't try to do everything at once, because if you're tired it's no fun." On hot days, it's a good idea to get your hand stamped, leave the parks, and go back to the hotel for lunch or a swim.

Plan each day by choosing the best time to see each attraction. To avoid the longest lines, follow the advice in the theme park tips that begin on the next page. Try to be flexible, and allow extra time in the schedule for surprises.

On the opposite page, there's some space for you to begin writing your family's schedule.

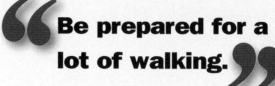
MAGIC KINGDOM TIPS

• Head to the Magic Kingdom first, since it's the park with the most rides for kids.

• Get to the park early so you're at the end of Main Street when the rest of the park opens.

• Check the Tip Board at the end of Main Street. It tells you how long the wait is for the most popular attractions.

• You won't have to wait as long if you go to Space Mountain, Alien Encounter, Splash Mountain, Big Thunder Mountain, Pirates of the Caribbean, and Fantasyland either first thing in the morning or during the 3 P.M. parade.

• Another great time to visit the top attractions is at night, during or after the SpectroMagic parade. You can sometimes get right on the rides without waiting very long.

• If there are two lines, the one on the left is almost always shorter.

• Never eat before riding Space Mountain, Splash Mountain, or Big Thunder Mountain Railroad.

• Don't be afraid to go on Big Thunder Mountain Railroad unless you really hate roller coasters. Avoid Splash Mountain if you don't like big drops.

• There are several "chicken exits" in the line for Space Mountain, so you can change your mind at the last minute.

• Save time for souvenir shopping on Main Street.

If you want to see an attraction more than once, try it again after dark when lines are usually shorter.

152

EPCOT TIPS

• Start your day at Test Track (which opens in the spring). Then go to the Wonders of Life pavilion to ride Body Wars and see Cranium Command. If there's time, see Honey, I Shrunk the Audience at the Journey Into Imagination pavilion.

• Head over to World Showcase when it opens at 11 A.M. Go back to Future World in the afternoon when it's less crowded.

• Remember: Most of Future World closes at 7 P.M. But Innoventions and Spaceship Earth stay open later.

• Check the digital Tip Board in Innoventions Plaza. It tells you how long the wait is for many attractions.

• Save time for all the interactive exhibits at Innoventions, Image Works, The Living Seas, and Wonders of Life.

• Don't miss the Leap Frog Fountains outside the Journey Into Imagination pavilion.

• Take a guided tour of the countries in World Showcase in the Wonders of the World program. See pages 144 and 145 for details.

• Buy a passport at any World Showcase shop and get it stamped in every country. It's a great reminder of your trip.

• Try not to see the movies at Canada, France, and China all in a row.

• Take time to talk to the people who work in World Showcase. Most of them come from the country of the pavilion they represent, and they have many interesting stories to tell.

• The best place to watch IllumiNations is from the little island between Italy and The American Adventure.

DISNEY-MGM STUDIOS TIPS

• Arrive at the Disney-MGM Studios before the posted opening time. The gates usually open about a half hour before the scheduled time.

• The character breakfast at the Soundstage restaurant is a great way to start the day.

• Tower of Terror has very long lines. See it early in the day and never right after a meal.

• See Muppet*Vision 3-D, Voyage of the Little Mermaid, and Star Tours in the morning before the lines get too long.

• There is one "chicken exit" at Tower of Terror, right before you get on the ride elevator, just in case you change your mind at the last minute.

• Some attractions don't open until late morning. Be sure to check your guidemap for exact showtimes.

• Check the Tip Board at the end of Hollywood Boulevard. It tells you which attractions are about to begin a new show, and which have the shortest lines.

• Get a good spot along Hollywood Boulevard to see the afternoon parade.

• Don't miss the newest attraction, Disney's The Hunchback of Notre Dame—A Musical Adventure.

MORE TIPS

- Try to eat lunch early in the day. Then you can go on rides while everyone else is eating and the lines are shorter.
- Once you have seen the three theme parks, check out the water parks and the Wonders of the World programs.

- Bring rain ponchos or an umbrella because you never know when it will rain. You can also buy bright yellow Mickey ponchos all around Walt Disney World.
- Do your shopping at the Disney Village Marketplace.
- If you like gum, bring your own. It's not sold anywhere at Walt Disney World.

Where the Lines Are

Some attractions tend to have long lines. The kids say some are worth waiting for. Others are lots more fun when they're less crowded. Use the list below to help you decide if you want to get in line.

Worth the Wait
- Space Mountain
- Splash Mountain
- Big Thunder Mountain Railroad
- Test Track
- The Twilight Zone Tower of Terror
- Pirates of the Caribbean
- Legend of The Lion King
- Cranium Command

- Body Wars
- Star Tours
- Jim Henson's Muppet*Vision 3-D
- Honey, I Shrunk the Audience
- Alien Encounter

Try Again Later
- It's A Small World
- Mad Tea Party
- Skyway
- Jungle Cruise
- Spaceship Earth
- Journey Into Imagination Ride
- Voyage of the Little Mermaid
- Country Bear Jamboree
- Dumbo, the Flying Elephant

TRAVELING WITH YOUR FAMILY

If you follow our hints for working out a schedule with your parents and brothers and sisters before you go, it will be easier to include something for everyone.

Remember that your parents are looking forward to this vacation as much as you are. Lissy warns, "Don't try to force your parents to do things that will make them unhappy because they will act unhappy." But don't worry, as Nita says, "No matter how old you are, you'll always love Walt Disney World."

Here are a few hints to help everyone get along:

• Go to the most popular attractions early in the day so you don't argue about waiting in long lines. To ride the best attractions a second time, wait and go during a parade or at night, when the rides are less crowded.

• Your parents will want to see the movies in World Showcase at Epcot. Plan your day so you begin at the best Future World pavilions, like Test Track (opening in the spring) and Wonders of Life (with Body Wars and Cranium Command). Later on head for the countries with the movies. Remember, you have to stand for the movies in Canada and China. You get to sit down for the France movie. A good way to break up the movies is to go on the boat ride in Norway.

"Get a lot of rest, because if you're exhausted you can't do anything."

Brian L. (age 12)

• Talk your parents into taking a break for ice cream or another snack in the late afternoon. Everyone gets tired of walking, so a cool drink or snack is refreshing.

• Have your entire family wear the same hat or shirt color so it's easy to stay together.

• The kids agree that Walt Disney World is more fun when you're there with other kids. Bring your younger brothers and sisters (ages 2 to 7) to the Magic Kingdom. They'll really like Mickey's Toontown Fair; It's A Small World; Cinderella's Golden Carrousel; Dumbo, the Flying Elephant; and the Country Bear Jamboree. For kids who might be afraid of the dark, avoid Peter Pan's Flight, Snow White's Adventures, Pirates of the Caribbean, Mr. Toad's Wild Ride, and especially The Haunted Mansion and Alien Encounter. At the Disney-MGM Studios, the kids think they'd like to play with younger siblings at the Honey, I Shrunk the Kids Movie Set Adventure playground.

• If you're an older kid, you might want to split up from your parents for a while. Agree on a meeting time and place, and don't get in any long lines too close to your set time. Don't meet at Cinderella Castle—it's too crowded.

• If you turn around and your parents have disappeared, or if they don't show up at your agreed-upon meeting place, you should go to Baby Services or City Hall in the Magic Kingdom, Guest Relations near Innoventions or Baby Services next to the Odyssey Center in Epcot, or Guest Relations near the front gate at the Disney-MGM Studios. Just ask a park employee and he or she will point you in the right direction.

The best way to find the characters is to check the park guidemap.

WHERE TO FIND THE CHARACTERS

Check a theme park guidemap to find out where and when you can find your favorites. Mickey and his pals visit all three parks throughout the day. You can say hello and maybe even take a picture with them. It's also fun to get the characters to autograph either a special autograph book or inside the back cover of this book. See how many you can collect!

Magic Kingdom: Join Cinderella for breakfast at King Stefan's and meet Goofy for dinner at the Liberty Tree Tavern. Or try a meal at the Crystal Palace with Winnie the Pooh and Tigger, too.

More characters appear next to City Hall throughout the day. Everyone gets a turn to meet them and have a photo taken. Rafiki and Timon often hang out at the entrance to Adventureland. Alice and her pals from Wonderland are sometimes in Fantasyland, while Brer Fox and Brer Bear enjoy spending time at Splash Mountain.

By far the best place to find characters is Mickey's Toontown Fair. Meet Mickey and Minnie in their country homes, and the rest of the gang under the big tent.

Epcot: In Future World, meet Chip 'n' Dale at the character meals at the Garden Grill restaurant. They stop at each table so you can get pictures. Mickey and pals appear at the Centorium shop. Rafiki and Timon spend time in The Land pavilion, and Sport Goofy can sometimes be spotted at Wonders of Life. Dreamfinder and Figment drop by Journey Into Imagination.

In World Showcase, you can greet Mickey and his closest pals at The American Adventure. You might find Belle and Beast near France, Jasmine and Aladdin in Morocco, and Snow White in Germany. But the best spot for character sightings is the United Kingdom. Alice and the White Rabbit, Peter Pan and Captain Hook, Winnie the Pooh, and Mary Poppins all hang out here at different times during the day.

Disney-MGM Studios: The Soundstage restaurant is the place to meet your favorite characters from the latest animated movies, like *The Hunchback of Notre Dame*, *Aladdin*, *Beauty and the Beast*, and *Pocahontas*. Enjoy the buffet any time of day.

If you want to meet Mickey, don't go looking for him on Mickey Avenue. He greets visitors on Sunset Boulevard. There, you can line up to pose for a picture.

So who's on Mickey Avenue? Lots of the other characters, like Woody and Buzz Lightyear, pass through here all the time. So keep a lookout for them. Go in the afternoon when there aren't as many people, and you can get a ton of pictures.

Disney Lingo

Audio-Animatronics:
Lifelike figures, from birds and hippos to movie stars and presidents. They seem so real—even though they're not.

Buffeteria:
The Disney word for cafeteria.

Cel:
The actual painted film used in an animated movie.

Guidemap:
A theme park map that also describes attractions, shops, restaurants, and entertainment.

Imagineer:
The Disney name for a creative engineer who designs theme park attractions.

TIPS FOR TAKING PICTURES

- In each park there are Photo Spots marked by little signs with cameras on them. Photos taken from these places will turn out best.
- It's fun to bring your own disposable camera. These cameras are easy to use and carry, and you'll have your own pictures to paste in this book as a reminder of your trip.
- Bring lots of film.
- Make sure your fingers aren't in front of the lens.
- Don't shoot too close or too far away from your subject.
- You cannot take pictures inside the attractions.

- Your parents will probably take lots of pictures of you with the characters. It's also fun to take pictures of your parents with *their* favorite characters.

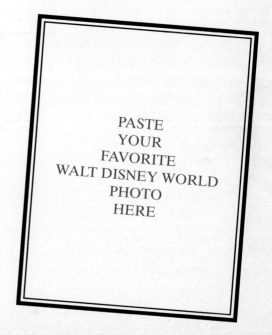

PASTE
YOUR
FAVORITE
WALT DISNEY WORLD
PHOTO
HERE